> grids <

veruschka götz

> grids <

for the **internet**

and other

digital media

AVA Publishing SA
Switzerland

Sterling Publishing Co., Inc.
New York

An AVA Book
Published by AVA Publishing SA
rue du Bugnon 7
CH-1299 Crans-près-Céligny
Switzerland
Tel: +41 78 600 5109
Email: enquiries@avabook.ch

Distributed by Thames and Hudson (ex-North America)
181a High Holborn
London WC1V 7QX
United Kingdom
Tel: +44 20 7845 5000
Fax: +44 20 7845 5050
Email: sales@thameshudson.co.uk
www.thamesandhudson.com

Distributed by Sterling Publishing Co., Inc.
in USA
387 Park Avenue South
New York, NY 10016-8810
Tel: +1 212 532 7160
Fax: +1 212 213 2495
www.sterlingpub.com

in Canada
Sterling Publishing
c/o Canadian Manda Group
One Atlantic Avenue
Suite 105, Toronto
Ontario M6K 3E7

English Language Support Office
AVA Publishing (UK) Ltd.
Tel: +44 1903 204 455
Email: enquiries@avabooks.co.uk

ISBN 2-88479-003-9

10 9 8 7 6 5 4 3 2 1

Design by Veruschka Götz

English translation by Victor Dewsbery, Berlin
and Richard Holmes, Berlin

Production and separations
by AVA Book Production Pte. Ltd., Singapore
Tel: +65 6334 8173
Fax: +65 6334 0752
Email: production@avabooks.com.sg

> grids <

for the **internet**
and other
digital media

introduction 008

1.0

constructing a grid 016

1.01 **paper formats** | 018
1.02 **choice of typefaces** | 020
1.03 **width and distance of columns** | 026
1.04 **columns** | **type area** | 028
1.05 **columns** | **leading** | 034
1.06 **classical gridspaces** | 036
1.07 **extra elements in a grid** | 038

2.0

rules for the screen 042

2.01 **colour systems for the screen** | 044
2.02 **colours and their effect** | 048
2.03 **choice of typefaces** | 052
2.04 **line length** | **text quantity** | 060
2.05 **line spacing** | **word spacing** | 062
2.06 **type sizes** | 068

content

3.0

grids for the screen 070

3.01 **consequences for grid design** | 072
3.02 **programming languages** | 076
3.03 **flow charts – how to structure a concept** | 078
3.04 **structures for the screen** | 084
3.05 **distribution on a screen** | 094
3.06 **layout elements** | 096
3.07 **innovative grid solutions** | 098
3.08 **dos and don'ts** | 114
3.09 **front pages** | 122
3.10 **banners** | 126
3.11 **cd-roms** | 128
3.12 **mini-screens** | 132

4.0

transfer of grids 134

4.01 **comparison: print, cd-rom, internet** | 136
4.02 **examples: print, cd-rom, internet** | 138

index:

literature | 146
quotations | 148
digital media | 150
print media | 154
typefaces | 155
catchwords | 156

introduction

>grids for the internet and other digital media<

1.0 **constructing a grid**

4.0 transfer of grids

2.0 rules for the screen

3.0 grids for the screen

introduction

introduction

Living in the Information Maze

Everybody regularly comes across chaotic websites, but these are not necessarily the products of screen-design pirates. Even major companies sometimes have presentations that are badly structured, hard to read and poorly signposted.

The user's search in this chaos is for clarity, convenience and reliability of the information that is provided – in this respect there is no real difference between paper and screen (or any digital display). But the screen provides a platform that is open for the self-presentation of any author, whatever their level of visual training, so that the presentations are increasingly becoming an impenetrable jungle of information.

The goal should be to provide users with a rapid overview of the information to hand. That means that the screen designer has to be able to establish an efficient hierarchy of information, with a clear layout and organisation.

A well thought-out grid system for the screens allows the screen designer to create this order, so that the recipients can easily orient themselves.

One of the key aspects of the design of typography and layouts is the work with grid systems. An intelligent grid provides a formal shape and structure, reduces user errors, and can make users curious about the information, and at the same time allows them to navigate through the datasets without losing their orientation. Good graphic design generates a visual logic and strives for the ideal balance between producing visual sensations and passing on contents.

Visual and functional continuity in the organisation of screen design, graphic design, and typography are important when it comes to convincing the recipient that the content is useful and relevant.

The content and the menus should be carefully structured so that it is easy to register what is being offered, to find things quickly, and then download files without difficulty. The organisation of information and hierarchies, a uniform editorial style, graphic and text-based overviews and suitable summaries are just as much elements of a grid system as clear icons, graphic identity schemes, and the logical structure and unity of modules that can be used repeatedly. The goal is to be consistent and at the same time introduce variety within the grid structure. (A good grid should not restrict but enable identity and freedom.) When the recipient has understood and learnt to read a grid, it becomes easy to explore a website.

Many of the rules from typesetting and the principles of page layout in printing cannot simply be transferred to screen design: For example the screen requires the use of a larger font size because of its poorer resolution, and requires landscape layouts in contrast to the portrait format of most printed pages, the orientation and navigation is also different. Adaptations are necessary to suit the different conditions of the new medium. But the screen designer must go beyond this and plan grids without expecting the precision provided by print media. Differing hardware and software arrangements affect the appearance of the screen, making it important to use an extended approach to grids, with more use of colours or navigation elements to arrange structures than is necessary with print media.

»Grids for the Internet and other Digital Media« considers key aspects of the adaptations that need to be taken into consideration when designing grid structures for the screen.

Legibility on screen

Type

Serif fonts are very good when text is printed
on paper. But on screen sans serif fonts are better,
because they don't have as many fine lines so are
clearer and create fewer pixel effects.

Every font has its own individual character,
and this has to be taken into account when
choosing a font for a publication.

chapter 1

Lufthansa
chapter 2

Nice work
chapter 4

The same rule applies for colours as for
typography, added features or animations:
use only as much as you need rather than as
much as possible.

Typographical grid elements

chapter 1

chapter 2

A font size of at least 10 pt should be used for text
on screen in order to make sure that it can be read
easily.

A patterned background requires a larger font
size than a plain background. There should be a
clear colour contrast between the type and the
background to ensure legibility.

chapter 2

The interaction of the elements:
The column width, lengths, and margins all
contribute towards producing text which is
easy to read.

Colours

The RGB-colour model
is the basis for digital media.
The CMYK-colour model
is the basis for print media.

chapter 2

Colours have different significance in different
cultures. The designer has to take that into
account when choosing colours.

The effects of colours interact with each other.
For the designer it is very important to ensure
appropriate contrast.

chapter 2

chapter 2

If italic styles, highlighting forms or experimental fonts are to be used on screen, care must be taken to ensure that the type size is large enough and that these fonts are only used for individual words or logos. Due to the extremely poor resolution, they should never be used for copy text.

Not all font styles are suitable for the screen. Ultralight and light styles are not suitable for the screen because the lines are too thin for the pixels unless the type is used in very large type sizes. Italic styles and narrow letter spacing should also be avoided. Normal, expanded and bold type styles are very suitable. With bold type, the lines should not be too thick because this could make the letters run together. To ensure good legibility, the letter spacing should be wider, but this has the disadvantage of creating an ungainly impression.

chapter 2

chapter 2

chapter 2

To transform a heavily pixel-based type display into clearly legible text, the steps can be artificially »smoothed«.

In order to make text on screen easier to read the lines have to be spaced further apart than is needed on paper. If we assume that 35 characters per line are ideal to read on screen, the line spacing should be 130–150% of the solid type. The longer the line is, the greater the line spacing that is needed for the text. Wide and thin type styles need a greater line gap, whereas narrow and bold styles need less.

For optimum legibility, columns on paper should only have up to ten words, or 35 to 55 keystrokes. On the screen, however, the column width (or line length) should not be more than 35 keystrokes, even though the horizontal format of the screen actually seems to encourage long lines.

If text is set in a single column on screen, then it is necessary either to keep the column narrow, or to increase the font size, in order to make sure that there aren't too many words per line. If there is too much text, due to the poor screen resolution it will be hard to read.

chapter 2

chapter 2

chapter 2

chapter 2

chapter 3

The fine positioning of text blocks is not always possible when it comes to balancing web pages. Depending on the browser and the user configuration, the elements can appear in different positions on the screen, and so text is positioned further left, in order to avoid over-hanging text being chopped off on the right side of the screen.
An exception are pages that open in a separate window or are positioned against a generous background.

The colour schemes of digital media cost nothing to use, in contrast to print media. As a designer it is advisable to make careful use of colour if the design is not to end up looking kaleidoscopic.

Striking colour contrasts should not be used on information websites because this makes reading more difficult. But, they can be very useful as an eye-catcher on start pages.

chapter 3

Colours are ideal for establishing and arranging a matrix without intricate structures, and to create links.

Grids

Functional elements that can always be found in the same position on a grid help the users to explore freely without having to worry about losing track of where they are.

Due to the differences in hardware and software between users, the »classical« grid from the world of printing has to be extended to include additional parameters in order to provide visual and functional continuity.

When designing digital screen presentations it is not only important to take into account the specific properties offered by the media – like animation, interaction, and the flexibility of the presentations in contrast to the permanence of print media – elements which are also used in printed matter must be adapted for use on screen. For example, the low resolution of the screen and its landscape format make it necessary to have a number of narrow columns so that the text is easier to read.

A grid cannot be transferred exactly from one medium to another. If the designer chooses »quotations« of the typical colours, pictures or typography of one medium and transfers them to the other medium, this maintains the aesthetic impression and thus the recognition value.

Function and hierarchy grid
Standard arrangement and coding of functional elements such as navigation bars and the orientation guides.
Colour grid
Definition of functions and areas by use of colour.
Sound grid
Definition of interactions by sound.
Movement and time grids
Action and speed of moving objects.
Quotation grid
Fixed images with text and illustration, which cannot be altered by user settings.
Aesthetic grid
The unchanging character of presentation of a website.

For print publications, the designer can choose freely between portrait and landscape, although the portrait orientation is more common.
But when it comes to designing digital media, the screen requires the use of a landscape orientation.

An impressive presentation is best achieved by choosing an asymmetrical array of functional elements in the grid. Too much symmetry can seem clumsy, inflexible and boring.

A site should not be overloaded, but neither should it be patchy and uneven. The designers should take care to ensure that not more than five to seven elements are included on any one page.

For example, a hierarchical arrangement might involve the use of different sizes (large/small), animations (moving/still), or a suitable colour scheme.

Using flow charts (miniatures of the sequences and the distribution) it is possible to get an overview of text and pictures for each page. This can be a big help when it comes to determining the grid.

Rollovers, pull-down menus and pop-up windows are typical interactive elements that can be used to make a lot of space and improve the overall screen structure.

Navigation

In order to determine the grid for a website, it is best to position the »functional elements« first, for example the navigation bar. The remaining space is then freely available for other purposes.

Every page should have a navigation element, this helps with the orientation and gives the user the certainty of being able to move backwards and forwards and jump about without getting lost. Feedback and orientation aids, including graphics, icons or short summaries also form important elements of a good navigation structure.

Too many navigation bars can make the overall structure appear restless, and can hinder visual guidance as opposed to helping it. Therefore, there should be no more than two bars.

Full-screen navigation is only suitable for individual pages. Repeated exposure to large selections of interactive options would end up confusing the user.

Feedback and orientation aids, including graphics, icons or short summaries also form important elements of a good navigation structure. An attractive website should offer logical and predictable connections, though it can include surprises when it comes to the detail.

Digital media are regarded as modern, dynamic means of communication. Users expect that the texts should also be fresh and lively, and that the labels used, for example for links, should be short and easy to understand.

In most cases the start-up page will be the first thing that a user sees of a website. It can be purely visual, containing only essential information, much like the cover of a book, or it can be more like the front page of a magazine, with information about key items of content.

The linear grid includes a navigation bar as a standard element. The only thing there that changes is the selected information, and this is the interesting feature of a website.

Fluid Grids: A flexible structure is not synonymous with lack of structure. The grid constants can be related to a system of colour codes and repeating elements, which always work according to the same pattern and thus establish a functional and aesthetic unity.

A grid at various levels: the basic structure remains the same, whereas the information in the navigation part and information part can be exchanged depending on the interaction.

Mini-screens do not offer much space for a clear grid structure, particularly if colour is not available as a code for functions. The designer can make use of »traditional« symbols for the functions, and although these might not seem sharp because of the poor resolution, they will be readily identified. Another option is to develop abstract symbols which look good, but then these will have to be learnt by the users.

Maximum pixel dimensions for print-out
Width 535 | Height 295 pixels

Maximum pixel dimension for use exclusively on the computers
Width 595 | Height 295 pixels

The navigation bar is positioned to the left. This corresponds to most people's reading habits, but given that users will be using all sorts of monitors, it also ensures that no items are off-screen.

A central vertical navigation bar, like a central horizontal bar, is suitable for pages with low information content and a lot of pictures, or only short texts.

An alternative to a vertically arranged navigation bar is the horizontal bar. A horizontal navigation bar leaves more space for information within the navigation area, but it has the disadvantage that it can impair the overall structure of the website if it is arranged in the centre.

A navigation bar at the bottom of the screen leaves a lot of space for pictures and text, and directs attention towards the information. But it is important to make sure that the navigation is not simply overlooked. On the other hand, the navigation points should be kept as brief as possible so that the page does not seem bottom heavy.

If the intention is to irritate the user, then elements can be placed bottom right, for example, but then they should be animated in order to attract attention to them in this unexpected position.

Limited scrolling can help to keep things clear, and will make it easier to navigate. As an alternative to scrolling, information can be provided on a number of pages.

1.0 constructing a grid

introduction

basics:
typography & colour

2.0 rules for the screen

1.0 constructing a grid

1.01 paper formats | 018
1.02 choice of typefaces | 020
1.03 width and distance of columns | 026
1.04 columns | **type area** | 028
1.05 columns | **leading** | 034
1.06 classical gridspaces | 036
1.07 extra elements in a grid | 038

4.0 transfer of grids
from print to screen

3.0 grids for the screen

1.01 Constructing a grid
Paper formats
Dimensions and orientation

Before the grid can be developed, it is necessary to determine the format and choose the orientation – either portrait or landscape.

For print publications, the designer can choose freely between portrait and landscape, although the portrait orientation is more common. But when it comes to designing digital media, the screen requires the use of a landscape orientation.

Paper formats: first things first

Before a layout is designed, the designer must first determine the exact purpose that the layout must fulfil. He then chooses a paper format to fit the purpose. The format is often determined by economic, printing and postal considerations, and these often lead to a size based on the DIN format (DIN = Deutsche Industrie Norm/German industry standards). The DIN format, which is one of the most frequently used paper size standards, became a standard format for German business and public authority stationery in 1922. It defines a series of formats that are derived from an area of one square metre and designed so that halving the long side produces the next smaller format. The advantage of using DIN formats is that paper manufacturers always have these

formats in stock, printing and cutting machines are designed for them, postage prices are based on them and they are easy to archive in files and other means of storage.
The disadvantage of the DIN formats is that they can quickly appear boring, so if the paper format is not yet defined it is advisable to experiment with the proportions. An elongated horizontal format is much more attractive than a format with sides of equal length. But by an imaginative, i. e. not symmetrical sub-division of the space, the designer can even create an interesting format with equal sides (**1**.1, **1**.2).

1.1

1.2

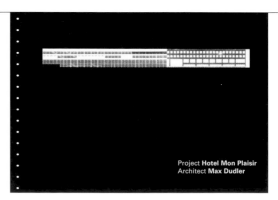

2.1

The format A0 has an area of 1m². The side ratio of the DIN formats is 5:7 or 1√2 (1:1.4114). In the ISO A series of paper sizes, each format has one side length in common with the next larger or smaller size.

The A series formats are the most common end formats, the B series are the untrimmed formats and the C series are the envelopes and packaging for the A series.

DIN Formats I in mm

	A	B	C
0	841 x 1189	1000 x 1414	917 x 1297
1	594 x 841	707 x 1000	648 x 914
2	420 x 594	500 x 707	458 x 648
3	297 x 420	353 x 500	324 x 458
4	210 x 297	250 x 353	229 x 324
5	148 x 210	176 x 250	162 x 229
6	105 x 148	125 x 176	114 x 162
7	74 x 105	88 x 125	81 x 114

Other formats I in mm

English poster format (double crown)	640 x 1020
World poster format	905 x 1280
US letter	216 x 279,5
US letter long	216 x 355,5

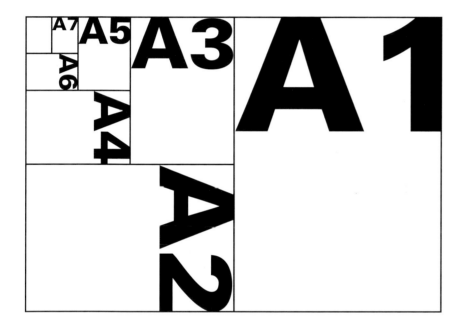

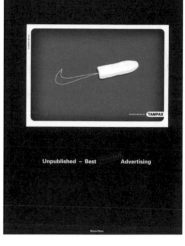

Format (1:√3)   Format DIN A4 (1:√2)

1.1, 1.2
By an imaginative sub-division of the space, the designer can even create an interesting format with equal sides. Formats with equal sides do not necessarily have to appear boring.

2.1
Architects like to produce their plans for clients on A3 format. But they forget that their clients often only have a normal briefcase with them and that the document must be rolled up to fit into it. It is easy to imagine what it will look like when it is later removed from the briefcase.

»[...], who have ideas, but are unable to organise them, like those barbarian generals who lead whole hosts of Persians or Huns into battle and fight as chance may come, but without order, without coherence and therefore without any result.«
Eugène Delacroix

1.02 Constructing a grid
Choice of Typefaces
Serif and sans serif fonts

The designer can determine the effect created by a publication with the choice between a serif or sans serif font.

Serif fonts are very good when text is printed on paper, but on screen sans serif fonts are better, as they do not have as many fine lines so appear clearer and less pixelated.

Serif Bauer Bodoni

wolf

Sans serif Univers 55

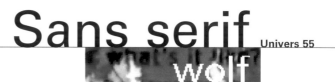

wolf

Typefaces

To design a good grid it is important for the designer to have sufficient knowledge of the semantic effect of typefaces in order to choose an appropriate font. There is an enormous and confusing variety of typefaces on the market, and much skill is needed to select a suitable typeface. The designer must have a clear concept of the desired visual appearance, and this should be derived from the function of the text. The functional, aesthetic and psychological impact of the type must be appropriate for the recipient and the content, and the »personality« of each possible typeface must also be taken into account.

Fundamentally, typefaces can be sub-divided into two forms: serif typefaces and sans serif typefaces.

The serif typefaces are typefaces with pronounced serifs and distinct differences between the thickness of the lines. These elegant looking typefaces are often used for newspaper and book printing because of their good legibility.

Sans serif typefaces are typefaces with no differences, or only slight differences, in the line thickness. These typefaces, with their sober and rational appearance, are used for head-lines, titles, in advertising or as short text passages.

SLOW Univers 75

CONSERVATIVE Times New Roman

old Avantgarde

fast Univers 67, 57, 47

innovative SF Eccentric Opus

new Bodoni

Semantic expression of fonts ...

... which can also be used to irritate the reader.

»When I see beautiful type, wherever it may be,
even if I see the word ›Spielothek‹ set in the typeface Spielothek, I think:
that is beautiful.

Typography is the letter in its multitude of forms,
a marvellous,
enormous aesthetic expanse on the page.«

Rainald Goetz

The selection of fonts and their positioning can be used to tell typographic stories: the character of Adam and Eve and their relationship is different in the two examples shown.

| **light** | Helvetica 95 | eva fey | Futura | *eve* ADAM | **Apple Chancery** **Formata Bold** |
| heavy | Helvetica 25 | **eva fey** | Old English | | **Garamond** **Remedy Double** |

The name Eva Fey can be expressed differently through the choice of font. If she is modern then a Futura is more appropriate than the old-fashioned Old English.

1.02 **Constructing a grid**
Choice of Typefaces
The nature of fonts

Every font has its own individual character, and
this has to be taken into account when choosing
a font for a publication.

Garamond   Humanists and Garaldes | Claude Garamond (1480–1561)

Garamond is a serif typeface
which can be classified as
Renaissance old style. It is
characterised by its thin serifs
which give the typeface a fine
appearance. This typeface is
very legible and makes the
text look bright and spacious.
It is used for texts which aim
for an attractive appearance
without the character of a
classical old style typeface.

Apple Macintosh

Bodoni   Humanists and Garaldes | Gianbattista Bodoni (1740–1813)

Bodoni is also a serif typeface.
It is one of the best known and
most widespread classical old
style typefaces.
The thin hairlines contrast
strongly with the thick stems.
Texts set in vertical Bodoni
appear very elegant, gracious
and refined.
Bodoni should not be used in
very small sizes because of the
thin hairline strokes.

VOGUE

Times   Transitionals | Stanley Morison (1889–1967)

Times is a serif typeface which
can be classified as baroque old
style.
This typeface, with its short,
solid serifs was designed in 1923
by Stanley Morison for the
newspaper »The Times«.
Times was designed for newspaper printing and has a good
legibility even on poorer quality
paper in spite of its narrow letter
spacing. Times is easy to read
even in small type sizes and it
is therefore often used in fine
printing such as books and
contracts, and in the small
print in advertising campaigns,
all of which benefit from a
classical look.

»The typeface appeals even to the most conservative reader. [...]
A typeface which is to be successful in the present and
even in the future
must not be too ›different‹ or too ›distinctive‹.«
Stanley Morison

THE ﷽ TIMES
OF LONDON

On modern typography:
»[It] should match the technically designed forms of cars and planes,
based on a functional visual appearance,
without decoration and gimmicks.«
László Moholy-Nagy

Gill Sans   Lineales | Eric Gill (1892–1940)

The sans serif typeface Gill Sans was developed by Eric Gill at the end of the 1920s based on the »Underground Type« for the London underground designed by Edward Johnston. Gill Sans looks attractive and, with its clear and generously designed letters, it is easy to read when used for copy text. But it has a unique character with its distinctive capital R, M and Q and the small g.

frog design

Futura   Lineales | Paul Renner (1878–1956)

Futura, a sans serif linear old style which is one of the grotesque typefaces, was presented in 1926. Paul Renner gave the typeface a geometric formal structure which produces a very clear character. It appears very modern, elegant, unassuming and light.

This very frequently used typeface is particularly popular among architects – probably because of its geometric structure.

NEUHAUS

Helvetica   Lineales | Max Miedinger (1910–1980)

Helvetica, a sans serif linear old style which is one of the grotesque typefaces, was designed in 1957 by Max Miedinger. It was well received because it satisfied the desire for timeless design, and even today it is still one of the most successful grotesque typefaces. It appears neutral and rational and has a consistent and uniform visual character.

Due to its narrow letter spacing, Helvetica enables text to be distributed economically on the page.

Lufthansa

1.02 **Constructing a grid**
Choice of Typefaces
The nature of fonts

Clarendon Egyptienne | Fann Street Foundry (1845)

Clarendon is an Egyptian style typeface which can also be called a linear old style with serifs. This typeface, which is based on the classical old style, was presented in England in 1845. With its strong hairline strokes, it was designed as an alternative to the bold old style typefaces.
It was originally designed as a highlighting typeface for lexicographical use, but now it is also used in typewriters and as a forceful typeface in advertising. It is more suitable for headlines or slogans than for longer texts, which could appear more like a manuscript because of the effect of the typeface.

Trixie Plain Experimental style | Erik van Blokland (1967–)

The typeface Trixie, designed by Erik van Blokland in 1991, is an ironic reaction to the ever more perfect Postscript typefaces. Trixie, which is of course also available as a Postscript typeface, gives the impression of an old typewriter with its ragged and rough outlines.

Because of its individuality, the use of this typeface must be designed with careful attention to the effect and content.

Verdana Screen typeface | Lineales | Matthew Carter (1937–)

Verdana was developed especially for the display of texts on the screen. Even in small type sizes it is easily legible compared with other typefaces. The letters were developed from the pixel structure of the screen, not from the stroke of the pen like other typefaces.
This explains the good screen legibility, which is supported by the generous letter spacing of the typeface. Because of its elegance and fineness compared with other, heavier screen fonts, Verdana is not just used on the screen.

typoterror

»Wrong. Much too narrow – correct.
Somewhat too narrow – rhythmically correct.
Wrong. A jungle of letters. A common mistake – correct clear and beautiful.
Genuine – nonsense.«
Jan Tschichold on designing a typeface

Rotis Sans

The type family Rotis, designed by Otl Aicher in 1989, has the distinction of containing typefaces ranging from serif to sans serif:
Rotis Serif (serif), Rotis Semi Sans (semi serif), Rotis Semi (semi sans serif) and Rotis Sans (sans serif). The reference to different historical roots makes it difficult to classify Rotis as a whole in any category of type-faces.

The same applies to the two intermediate typefaces, Rotis Semi Sans and Rotis Semi Serif.

Kleimann & Partner

Rotis Semi Sans   Semi sans serif

If two typefaces from the Rotis family are to be combined, care must be taken not to select faces which are directly next to each other in the series, for example a combination of Rotis Sans and Rotis Semi Sans. The two intermediate types, Rotis Semi Sans and Rotis Semi Serif, should not be combined under any circumstances because they are too similar to each other.

ARCH⁺

Rotis Semi Serif   Semi Roman

The different typefaces in the Rotis type family are very similar in design. If the typefaces are combined, for example with the headline in Rotis Sans and the body text in Rotis Serif, this can preserve a uniform visual appearance of the type. The danger is that the type may appear too monotonous. Sometimes, a greater visual tension can be created by combining typefaces which are completely different.
Because of the narrow letter spacing, the Rotis type family should not be used in small sizes (under 10 pt) because the text would appear cluttered, and this could impair legibility.

33.1 the lounge

1.03 Constructing a grid
Width and distance of columns
The interaction of the elements

Column widths, lengths, and margins all
contribute towards producing text which is
easy to read.

1.1

»But order, it seems, must be exceedingly simple.
It is full of experience [...], but in itself it must not show any gloom or
uncertainty as a result of experience.
Instead, it must be of the purest crystal.
But this crystal does not appear as an abstraction;
it is something concrete; the most concrete of things, almost the hardest.«

Ludwig Wittgenstein

1.2

**The elements of the grid
are closely interlinked in
their effect:**
Page format
Selection of typeface
Selection of type size
Leading
Edges of page | type area

Sub-division into columns:
40 to 50 letters per line are
regarded as ideal for body
text (see J. Müller-
Brockmann, Otl Aicher).

Long lines with more than 50
letters need greater leading,
so that the eye can find its
way more easily to the start
of the next line, but shorter
lines can manage without it.

Column width, gap between columns and column height

When you have selected a format and
chosen a typeface, the next step is to
create the grid. First of all, the column
width needs to be defined to enable the
text to be read easily. The type size is
closely linked with the column width.
For good legibility of texts, the column
should contain seven to ten words per
line (1.2). The language the text is written
in is also an important consideration:
German needs more space than Italian
or English (1.4). If the column is too wide
or too narrow, the reader tires quickly. If
a column contains more than ten words
per line, the text is more difficult to read
because the eye loses itself in the length
of the column (1.1). For very short texts,
however, there can be fewer words per
line without the text appearing fragmented (1.3). But narrow columns should not
be too long, because this impairs the
reader's concentration. If the columns
are too short on the other hand, the eye
is distracted and jumps to the next
column. As a designer you must use
your discretion to decide how long the
column should be; this depends on
elements which are closely related in
their effects: the column width, the
typeface, the type size and the correct
line spacing.

The leading (space between one line
and the next) is a very important
criterion which has a decisive effect
on the legibility of texts: If the leading
is too narrow, the text tends to »stick
together«, but if it is too wide this tends
to produce »white bars« between the
lines. The space between the letters
should always be slightly less than the
space between the lines. The leading
itself is closely linked with the gap
between columns. According to
Manfred Simoneit, the letters »mi« – in
the same typeface and type size as the
type in the column – should fit between
the columns. If the columns are separated by a line, at least »mii« should fit
between them (1.2).
If the leading for a text is large, this
»mi« rule no longer applies and the
gap between columns must be greater.
In fact, the value for the leading can be
transferred to the gap between columns.

1.3

1.4

Information Service

The contents of the ERCO
Internet servers are
constantly growing and
changing. If you would like

**The poor resolution of monitors
means that on-screen texts
can be read more easily if the
columns are narrower than are
usual on paper. But just as with
printed texts it is important to
make sure that narrow columns
are not too long.**

More than 20 words per line

When you have selected a format and chosen a typeface, the next step is to create the grid. First of all, the column width needs to be defined to enable the text to be read easily. The type size is closely linked with the column width. For good legibility of texts, the column should contain seven to ten words per line (**1.2**). The language the text is written in is also an important consideration: German needs more space than Italian or English (**1.4**). If the column is too wide or too narrow, the reader tires quickly. If a column contains more than ten words per line, the text is more difficult to read because the eye loses itself in the length of the column (**1.1**). For very short texts, however, there can be fewer words per line without the text appearing fragmented (**1.3**).

7–10 words per line

When you have selected a format and chosen a typeface, the next step is to create the grid. First of all, the column width needs to be defined to enable the text to be read easily. The type size is closely linked with the column width. For good legibility of texts, the column should contain seven to ten words per line (**1.2**). The language the text is written in is also an important consideration: German needs more space than Italian or English (**1.4**). If the column is too wide or too narrow, the reader tires quickly. If a column contains more than ten words per line, the text is more difficult to read because the eye loses

^{mi} itself in the length of the column (**1.1**). For very short texts, however, there can be fewer words per line without the text appearing fragmented (**1.3**). But narrow columns should not be too long, because this impairs the reader's concentration. If the columns are too short on the other hand, the eye is distracted and jumps to the next column. As a designer must use your discretion to decide how long the column should be; this depends on elements which are closely related in their effects: the column width, the typeface, the type size and the correct line spacing.

^{mii} The leading is a very important criterion which has a decisive effect on the legibility of texts: If the leading is too narrow, the text tends to »stick together«, but if it is too wide this tends to produce »white bars« between the lines. The space between the letters should always be slightly less than the space between the lines. The leading itself is closely linked with the gap between columns. According to Manfred Simoneit, the letters »mi« – in the same typeface and type size as the type in the column – should fit between the columns. If the columns are separated by a line, at least »mii« should fit between them (**1.2**).

4–5 words per line

When you have selected a format and chosen a typeface, the next step is to create the grid. First of all, the column width needs to be defined to enable the text to be read easily. The type size is closely linked with the column width. For good legibility of texts, the column should contain seven to ten words per line (**1.2**). The language the text is written in is also an important consideration: German needs more space than Italian or English (**1.4**).

with large leading

When you have selected a format and chosen a typeface, the next step is to create the grid. First of all, the column width needs to be defined to enable the text to be read easily. The type size is closely linked with the column width.

with small leading

When you have selected a format and chosen a typeface, the next step is to create the grid. First of all, the column width is defined to enable the text to be read easily. The type size is closely linked with the column width. For good legibility of texts, the column should contain seven to ten words per line (**1.2**). The language the text is written in is also an important consideration: German needs more space than Italian or English (**1.4**).

with no leading

The type size is closely linked with the column width.

english		german	
This is a text example that	6	Das ist ein Textbeispiel,	4
shows that a line of text	6	das beweist, dass in einer	5
in German contains fewer	4	Textzeile, die in deutsch	4
words than a line in English.	6	verfasst wurde, weniger	3
This is due to the large	6	Worte unterzubringen sind	3
numbers of compound words	4	als in einer, die in englisch	6
in German.	2	verfasst wurde. Das liegt	4
		daran, dass die deutschen	4
		Wörter zusammengesetzt	2
		sind und deshalb sehr lang	5
		werden können.	2

Gap between words and rows
Gap between words and rows

The line spacing for longer texts should always be somewhat larger than the spacing between the words, so that the lines are perceived as integral units.

The positioning of the text area on the page has
a crucial influence on whether a design appears to
be well-balanced.

Designing a type area

The area in which the text (or pictures)
appears is called the type page or type
area. The areas between the text (or
pictures) and the edge of the paper are
called the margins (1.1). In designing the
type page, care should be taken to
ensure a dynamic composition. If the
margins are too narrow, the page looks
cluttered and confusing. If the text is
too close to the edges, this can lead to
problems when the page is trimmed. In
newspapers, however, narrow margins
are used deliberately to accommodate as
much text as possible (2.1). If the margins
are too wide, the page looks wasteful
and the text can appear disjointed.
Here, too, there are exceptions when the
generous use of space is what is being
emphasised (2.2).

The fine positioning of text blocks is not
always possible when it comes to balancing
web pages. Depending on the browser and the
user configuration, the elements can appear in
different positions on the screen, and so text is
positioned further left, in order to avoid over-
hanging text being chopped off on the right side
of the screen. An exception to this are pages that
open in a separate window or are positioned
against a generous background.

1.1

2.1

2.2

»Organisation is crucial to life.«
German proverb

3.1
If the top margin is too wide, the type area may seem to fall off the bottom of the page.

3.2
If the top margin is too narrow, the type area may seem to fall off the top of the page.

3.3
If the proportional distribution of the margins is too even, the page appears harmonious, but it can quickly become boring.

3.4
A good arrangement of the type area: the proportions of the margins are in a dynamic relationship with each other.

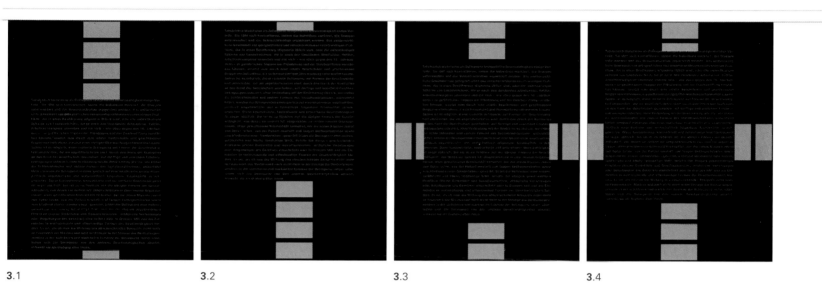

3.1   3.2   3.3   3.4

The type area of a single page can have the same margins at the top, the outer edge and the inner edge, but the bottom margin should be larger, so that the text does not look as if it has slipped down the page. When a double page is designed, there should be a visual link between the type area of the right and left page (4.1).

The type areas must not be too far apart (4.2). There is a difference between the design of a type area for a single page and a double page, because in the latter the print layout has to form an optical unit.

4.1 (original)

4.2 (rearranged)

1.04 Constructing a grid
Columns | Type Area
Number of columns

The appropriate number of columns depends on the format, the font size, and above all on the function of the text.

1 column

»The need creates the form.«
Wassily Kandinsky

The more columns a type page has on each page, the less text can be fitted on the page.

Type area with multiple columns
When the format and typeface have been determined and the text volume and number of pictures are reasonably clear, the number of columns can be defined. The number of columns is closely linked with the format, the type size and especially the function of the text: Setting a novel with several columns per page would be very unusual, and setting a newspaper with a single column as wide as the newspaper page format would not only appear strange, but would be very difficult to read.
To avoid unreadable texts with more than 50 letters per line, the type area is divided into several columns. The type size and the different letter spacing values play an important role for the selection of the column width and thus the number of columns per page: with small type sizes and narrow letter spacing more characters fit into a line, and vice versa.

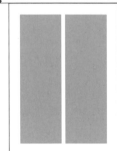

2 columns

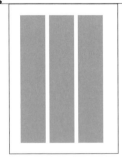

3 columns

If text is set in a single column on the screen, then it is necessary either to keep the column narrow, or to increase the font size, so that there are not too many words per line. If there is too much text, then it will prove hard to read as a result of the poor screen resolution.

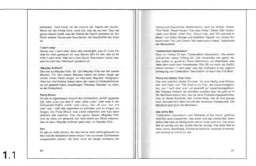
1.1

1.2

1.3

Single column type areas should not be wider than the normal paperback format unless the type size is large enough. Otherwise the lines can become too long, making it difficult for the reader to find the way back to the start of the next line. Single column type areas are used in literary works (1.1) such as novels or in introductory texts such as the preface (1.2). If the format is larger than A5, the type size in a single column type area must be increased accordingly (1.3).

The single column type area has the disadvantage that the designer has less freedom of design than with a more finely structured type area.

1.1 Mix, Cuts & Scratches: Format: 12 cm x 17 cm type size: 9 pt
1.2 Facts & Fakes: Format: 19,5 cm x 27 cm type size: 9 pt
1.3 Life Style: Format: 20,5 cm x 24,5 cm type size: 24 pt

2.1

2.2

A two column type area offers more opportunities: one column can be used for pictures, the other for text. The danger of two column type areas is that they can quickly become boring and lose their dynamic effect because of their symmetry. The designer can counter this by interestingly distributing pictures.

This two column format is used for larger formats.

2.1 Max Dudler: Format: 23,5 cm x 27,5 cm type size: 7 pt
2.2 Style magazine: Format: 24 cm x 32 cm type size: 7 pt

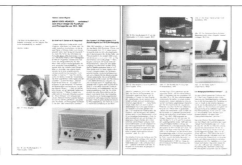
3.1

3.2   3.2

A three column grid is suitable for larger formats. It is often used in academic books, brochures and advertising.

3.1 Braun Design: Format: A4 type size: 10 pt
3.2 Program ilb: Format: 18,5 cm x 25,5 cm type size: 8 pt
3.3 Rejected: Format: A4 type size: 10 pt

1.04 Constructing a grid
Columns | Type Area
Number of columns

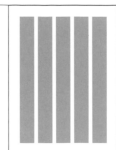

Less experienced designers
should begin with fewer
columns: a certain degree
of experience and sensitivity
is needed to handle the
diversity and flexibility of
multiple-column layouts.

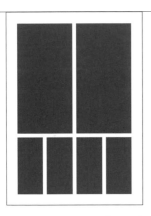

6.1

Every grid can also be varied within itself.
The individual columns can be sub-divided
as required. This increases the flexibility and
diversity of the design options.

6.1 The e-book: Format: 21,5 cm x 27,5 cm type size: 10 pt

»And there are more surprises in disorder than in order.
That is precisely what we mean by order:
that which is orderly can no longer surprise us.«
Tor Norretranders

Given the landscape orientation
of a monitor screen, then an
obvious option is to use a number
of columns. This also makes text
easier to read, because long lines
are harder to read on screen
than on paper.

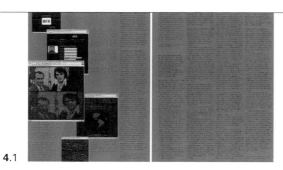

4.1

A four column type area is used if texts need to be read quickly, for example, in daily newspapers or magazines in which many short information reports are offered in compact form. A four column layout requires a very large page format.

4.1 Form: Format: 24 cm x 29,7 cm type size: 8 pt

5.1

A five column type area is a variant of the four column type area for large formats: it offers a high degree of flexibility and variability and has a particularly dynamic effect because of the odd number of columns.

5.1 Die Woche: Format: 31,5 cm x 47,3 cm type size: 10 pt

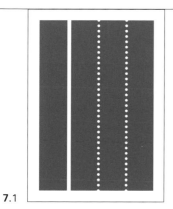
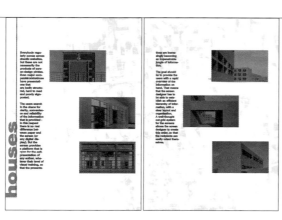
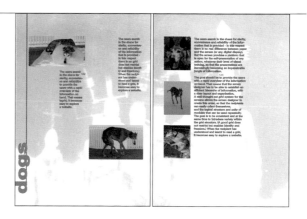

7.1

Pictures and text blocks do not always have to fit into a single column, but can also have double-column width from time to time.

7.1 Design Brochure: Format: A4 type size: 10 pt

8.1

Working without a grid as a stylistic choice: the label Gigolo Records uses the lack of a grid to create a deliberately unconventional and anarchistic effect.

8.1 The Great Gigolo Swindle: Format: A5 type size: 8 pt

1.05 Constructing a grid
Columns | Leading
Definition of the base line grid

By using a standard base line grid and fitting various font sizes into this grid, a tidy overall impression is created.

»The great style cannot do without the previously defined line.«

Eugène Delacroix

Base line grid

In publications, especially on white and thin paper, it is advisable for the margin between the type area on the left hand page and the left edge of the paper to be the same width as the margin between the type area on the right hand page and the right edge of the paper. This has the advantage that the margins will appear clear white, undisturbed by any printing on the reverse side. The same applies to the uniformity of a base line grid and the corresponding leading for basic texts: the lines of text in the type area on the left hand page should match the lines of text in the type area on the right hand page, in order to give the publication a uniform appearance.

The base line grid begins either at the top edge of the type area or at the top edge of the page. Different type sizes must be adapted to fit into the base line grid. The result is a clean and harmonious overall impression.

Before a column is defined, the leading should be decided on in order to determine the column height with the aid of the base line grid.

The red text lies exactly in the base line grid with an appropriate and easily legible leading. The line spacing in this case is 12 pt. The spacing of two lines is thus 24 pt, which means that the green text (on the right) rests on every second base line. The black text has line spacing of 8 pt and therefore rests on every third base line (24:3=8).

The green text (on the left) is exactly on the base line grid – without leading.

It wasn´t so very long ago that the term »anarchy« struck terror into the soul of the middle classes.

18 pt | Line spacing 12 pt

18 pt | Line spacing 24 pt

It wasn´t so very long ago tha terror into the soul of the mi of a society without control, a authority and accepted struct the Internet age the term ana radiating an aura of something desired. The Internet, a grass- a podium for free speech and opposed to existing hierarchi capital, authority, structures a

If authority is abandoned ther self-control to take over, whic lawlessness not only spawns a specific aims, but also intolera way the information is supplie Paradoxically, instead of enjoy experience the very lack of it is coded is a many-layered ma pient becomes lost.

In order to make text on screen easier to read the lines have to be spaced further apart than is needed on paper.

PHILOSOPHY

If the basic grid is identical on the front and reverse sides, then the space between the lines remains white, even if the paper is translucent, creating a clean, uniform impression.

10 pt | Line spacing 12 pt

It wasn't so very long ago that the term »anarchy« struck terror into the soul of the middle classes: fantasies were abound of a society without control, and of law and order, political authority and accepted structures being swept away. Today in the Internet age the term anarchy takes on a different meaning, radiating an aura of something positive, that which is desired. The Internet, a grass-roots evolution, a podium for free speech and an engine of democracy, stands opposed to existing hierarchies. It is against centralisation, capital, authority, structures and any game plan order.

If authority is abandoned then the stage is set for the illusion of self-control to take over, which aspires to no particular goal. This lawlessness not only spawns a mass of information lacking any specific aims, but also intolerable lawlessness in terms of the way the information is supplied and its aesthetic quality. Paradoxically, instead of enjoying a freedom newly won, we experience the very lack of it, because the way the information is coded is a many-layered maze in the middle of which the recipient becomes lost.

8 pt | Line spacing 8 pt

It wasn't so very long ago that the term »anarchy« struck terror into the soul of the middle classes: fantasies were abound of a society without control, and of law and order, political authority and accepted structures being swept away. Today in the Internet age the term anarchy takes on a different meaning, radiating an aura of something positive, that which is desired. The Internet, a grass-roots evolution, a podium for free speech and an engine of democracy, stands opposed to existing hierarchies. It is against centralisation, capital, authority, structures and any game plan order.

A grid cell structure gives a design a uniform feeling, and makes it easier to position text and pictures. The finer the cell structure the more flexible the designer can be.

»He who destroys form also damages the substance.«
Herbert von Karajan

»The dream of order is a legitimate dream, and it is beautiful.«
Peter Jenny

Cells in the grid

The vertical column arrangement can also be accompanied by a horizontal arrangement, thus creating a latticework of cells in the grid. Such a grid system requires a certain investment of time in planning, but this is made up for by the greater simplicity of the subsequent work and the time saved as a result.

To create a horizontal grid, the lines of the base line grid in the type area, minus the blank lines which separate the pictures, must be divided by the required number of cells in the grid. The result represents the number of lines per cell in the grid.

Pictures should not be aligned with the top edge of the type area because they may then protrude above the text. Therefore, the base line grid should be extended upwards by the height of the ascenders in the typeface.

8 cell grid

32 cell grid

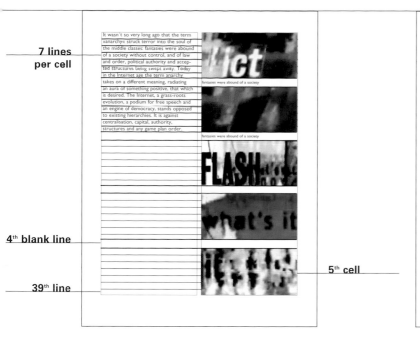

10 cell grid

15 cell grid with lines for the picture caption

Example »10 cell grid« :
39 lines - 4 blank lines = 35 »active« lines
35 : 5 cells in the grid = 7 lines per cell

Formula to calculate the number of lines per cell
Lines - blank lines = »active« lines
»Active« lines : cells in the grid = lines per cell

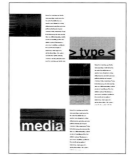

**The more grid cells then the more flexible
the designer can be: pictures and text can be
distributed variably over several grid cells.**

**Just as on paper, the grid cell
structure gives a design on
the screen a more harmonious
appearance.**

1.07 Constructing a grid
Extra elements in a grid
Headings and captions

When additional elements are fitted into the grid
they can support the overall aesthetic harmony.

Headlines

This headline is separated from
the text by two blank lines; one
line is often enough, and there
should never be more than two
blank lines. The headline matches
the typeface and type size of the
text. This variant is unobtrusive
and elegant and is not suitable for
use in sensationalist publications.

Headlines

This headline is set apart from the
text by a gap and is in keeping
with the type size of the text.
The style is slightly bolder than the
basic text. This variant has greater
contrast than the version on the
left, but it still looks elegant.

Headlines
This headline is not set apart from
the text by a gap and is the same
type size as the text. The style is
slightly bolder than the basic text.
This compact variant looks clear
but unobtrusive.

Headlines

If different type sizes are used, the
differences must be clearly recognisable. The greater the difference, the more striking the contrast
between the text and the headline
is. Heavily contrasted headlines
are a frequent stylistic device in
newspaper and magazine layout to
entice the reader to read the text.

Elements in the grid
Other elements which can be aesthetically included in a grid, apart from the basic
text and pictures, are page numbers,
headlines, sub-headings, marginal notes
and footnotes.
All these extra elements are generally
based on the typeface of the basic text,
although the size and style may differ.

headlines
Headlines can also be placed to
the side of the text and rotated
by 90 degrees. To do this, the
headline must have the character
of a slogan.
This unusual position for headlines
should not be excessively used, as
the overall impression otherwise
becomes erratic and the eye is
no longer guided.

Pierre Bonnard

What is true for paper is also true
for the monitor screen. But you
should make sure that the font
size used for the captions is not
too small, because on screen they
might easily become illegible.

grids
Visual and function
continuity in the o
screen design, gra
design, and typog
are imporwhen it c
to convincing the

Picture captions can be
aligned to the right or
left edge of the picture.
They should be flush
with the top or bottom of
the picture in order to
provide an optical link.

ПОСОЛЬСТВО РОССИИ

WEINHANDLUNG

The style of a picture
caption is often slightly
bolder than the basic text.
If the picture caption is long,
a narrower style can also be
used because the volume of
text should only exceed the
volume of the picture in very
exceptional cases – attention
should be focused on the
picture.

Usually the picture captions are placed under the
picture. The distance between the picture and the
caption corresponds to
the base line grid.

Headlines

Headlines can be set in a different typeface than the basic text.
In this case it is Helvetica Inserat combined with Times. This combination between a sans serif typeface and an serif typeface is often used.
If as a designer you want to create an unusual effect, you must be aware of typeface combinations.

HEADLINES

This headline is set in capitals. Other forms of highlighting such as underlining, kerning, spacing, use of colour etc. offer an infinite number of possible ways to distinguish a headline from the basic text. But such highlighting should not be used for the basic text.

Headlines

Headlines can also be placed to the side of the text.

Sub-headings
Sub-headings should be less prominent than the headline because they serve to sub-divide the text and help the reader to grasp the structure of the content at a glance.

Headlines

This headline is set in »Helvetica Bold Extended«, and the text is set in »Helvetica Roman«. The following sub-heading is in demi-bold Helvetica. The text is justified left and right.

sub-heading
The line spacing of the sub-heading is based on the base line grid for the sake of simplicity. This keeps the typesetting coherent and consistent.

HEADLINE

This headline is highlighted by »underlining«.

sub-heading
All forms of highlighting which are used for the headlines can also be used for the sub-headings. The effect should be less intense than the headline.

headlines

Headlines can also be placed to the side of the text. To do this, the headline must have the character of a slogan. This unusual position for headlines should not be excessively used, as the overall impression otherwise becomes erratic and the eye is no longer guided.

Headlines: Shorter headings can be placed in the text. This variant is used in publications which have limited space available, such as dictionaries and encyclopaedias.

Headlines

If headlines are centred above the text, the text itself should be justified left and right. That means that the start of the lines (left) and the ends of the lines (right) should be in a straight line. This is achieved by varying the spacing between the words. The other examples on this page are justified to the left only, in other words the lines form a straight line on the left and end in a jagged line on the right.

---

e-sense interactive KG

▸ Erscheinungsjahr: 1999
▸ Art der Website: Business to Business
▸ Aufgaben: Konzeption, Gestaltung und Programmierung der Website. Navigation, Animationen und Soundeffekte in Flash.
▸ Award: Flash-Site of the week
▸ URL: nicht mehr online

Contact.

Do you have any questions or would you like to make any comments? Please write to us! In addition to the departmental addresses listed here, you can contact any Wilkhahn member of staff direct, providing you know his/her name - and he/she is available through his/her computer. Just insert Name.Surname@wilkhahn.de and send it off.

■ **The Right Information To The Right People**
New technology developed by Relevare means that frustrations and wasted time associated with searching for information are now a thing of the past.

Whether the information you need is somewhere on your internal systems or out on the Web, Relevare have a combination of content delivery and software solutions that automates the task for organisations.

Bruce Mau Design, Inc.

1. Allow events to change you. You have to be willing to grow. Growth is different from something that happens to you. You produce it. You live it. The prerequisites for growth: the openness to experience events and the willingness to be changed by them.

The type size should be one, or better two point sizes smaller than the body copy, so that it can be seen as a sort of explanation of the body copy. The typeface need not be the same as the body copy, but it should be compatible with it.

If the **picture caption** is overlaid on the **picture**, there must be a clear contrast between the **text** and the picture.

1.07 Constructing a grid
Extra elements in a grid
Font styles, pagination, marginalia, and footnotes

Pagination, marginalia, and footnotes are extra elements which should always relate to the grid in order to ensure optical unity. Within this framework the designer can make use of other options, such as a different font size to draw attention to particular elements.

Type

A flexible design can be achieved with various sizes and styles.

2
Helvetica 23 Ultra Light Extended
Helvetica 24 Ultra Light Extended Italic
Helvetica 25 Ultra Light
Helvetica 26 Ultra Light Italic
Helvetica 27 Ultra Light Condensed
Helvetica 28 Ultra Light Condensed Italic

3
Helvetica 33 Thin Extended
Helvetica 34 Thin Extended Italic
Helvetica 35 Thin
Helvetica 36 Thin Italic
Helvetica 37 Thin Condensed
Helvetica 38 Thin Condensed Italic

4
Helvetica 43 Light Extended
Helvetica 44 Light Extended Italic
Helvetica 45 Light
Helvetica 46 Light Italic
Helvetica 47 Light Condensed
Helvetica 48 Light Condensed Italic

5
Helvetica 53 Extended
Helvetica 54 Extended Itali
Helvetica 55 Normal
Helvetica 56 Normal Italic
Helvetica 57 Condensed
Helvetica 58 Condensed Italic

Page numbers

A very common position: the page number is flush with the outer edge of the type area. Care should be taken to ensure that the page number is not isolated from the text or located outside the basic grid because otherwise the pagination seems optically to be more important than the text.

An unusual position: the page number is flush with the inner edge of the type area. This emphasises the central axis, the page number is less prominent and the layout appears more static than in the example on the left.

This central position below the text is a good solution for text justified left and right, and for publications which are read in a linear fashion, such as novels. It appears static and calm, and the page number is not obtrusive.

Marginal notes

The first line of a marginal note should be aligned with the first line of the basic text.

Marginal notes, which should be two point sizes smaller than the basic text (to distinguish them visually from the main text), are contained in a separate column which need not be as wide as the main text. Marginal notes are justified to the basic text and the first line should be aligned with the first line of the basic text, but the notes need not necessarily match the base line grid throughout. However, this is a good solution if the leading of the basic text permits, i.e. if it is not too great.

Footnotes

Footnotes in the text are denoted by small superscript characters such as asterisks* or numbers[1], and the footnote itself is found at the bottom of the page or the end of the book. Depending on the size of the main text, the footnote should be set at 6 to 8 pt.

* If the line is too long for the small type of the footnote, the footnotes can be sub-divided into several columns.

[1] Footnotes should be separated from the main text by at least one blank line.

»I dream of synthesis.
I conceive of the book as a uniform organism,
a magic crystal which is able
to unite all the lines of culture within itself.«
Pjotr Perevesenzev

7 Helvetica 73 Bold Extended
Helvetica 74 Bold Extended Italic
Helvetica 75 Bold
Helvetica 76 Bold Italic
Helvetica 77 Bold Condensed
Helvetica 78 Bold Condensed Italic

9 Helvetica 93 Black Extended
Helvetica 94 Black Extended Italic
Helvetica 95 Black
Helvetica 96 Black Italic
Helvetica 97 Black Compressed
Helvetica 98 Black Compressed Italic

6 Helvetica 63 Medium Extended
Helvetica 64 Medium Extended Italic
Helvetica 65 Medium
Helvetica 66 Medium Italic
Helvetica 67 Medium Condensed
Helvetica 68 Medium Condensed Italic

8 Helvetica 83 Heavy Extended
Helvetica 84 Heavy Extended Italic
Helvetica 85 Heavy
Helvetica 86 Heavy Italic
Helvetica 87 Heavy Condensed
Helvetica 88 Heavy Condensed Italic

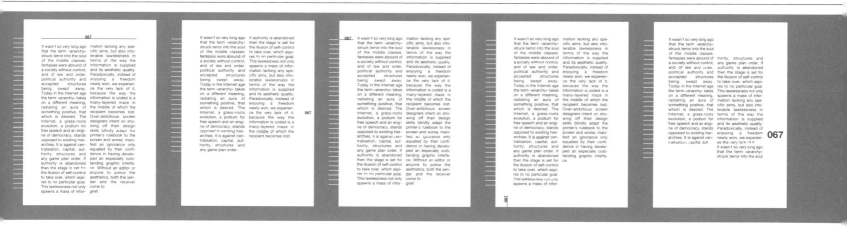

This central position above the text is a good solution for text justified left and right, and for publications which are used as reference works. This position enables the page to be found quickly.

Page numbers situated next to the type area should always be aligned with the base line grid.

Examples of how page numbers can be used as graphic elements.

Page numbers should be the same size as the basic text unless they are emphasised as a graphic element. The position of the page numbers depends on the type of publication: in magazines, newspapers and works of reference it is important for the themes to be found quickly. That means that the page numbers must be in a position where they are easily identified.

On websites there is usually no pagination, because the individual pages are mostly independent structures on different topics. Other orientation aids can be used instead – for example colour coding.

Different font styles.

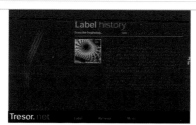

On the website of Eskedahl the topics are numbered.

2.0 rules for the screen
typography & colour

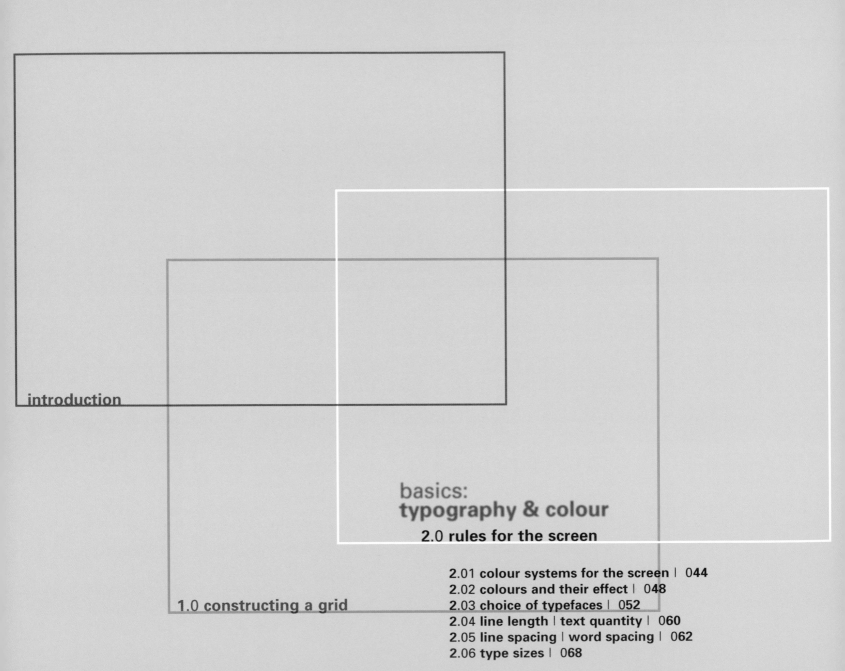

introduction

basics:
typography & colour
2.0 rules for the screen

1.0 constructing a grid

2.01 colour systems for the screen | 044
2.02 colours and their effect | 048
2.03 choice of typefaces | 052
2.04 line length | text quantity | 060
2.05 line spacing | word spacing | 062
2.06 type sizes | 068

3.0 grids for the screen

from print to screen

4.0 transfer of grids

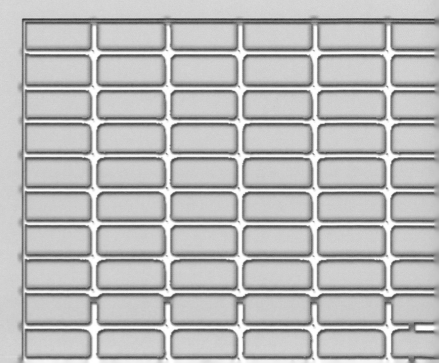

2.01 Rules for the screen
Colour systems for the screen
RGB and CMYK

The RGB-colour model is the basis for
digital media.
The CMYK-colour model is the basis for
print media.

»The painter of the future is a colourist, such as has never existed before.
This painter of the future –
I cannot imagine that he will hang
around in small bistros, have a mouth full of false teeth,
and visit Zouave bordellos like me.«

Vincent van Gogh

Too much colour can easily
seem overpowering. That might
be intentional in the case of an
extrovert website like the one
on the right. But a more careful use
of colour generally creates a more
trustworthy impression.

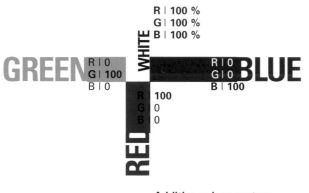

Additive colour system
Primary colours I red, green, blue

The additive colour system

The additive colour system is made up
of the primary colours: red, green and
blue (RGB). If these colours all occur in
equal intensity, this creates white, while
the absence of all three colours creates
black. Mixing two primary colours
produces the so-called secondary
colours: magenta, cyan and yellow.
If a primary colour is mixed with a
secondary colour, this produces a
tertiary colour.
Additive colour mixing is a physical-
optical operation with directly projected
light. The colours are displayed on the
screen on the basis of the RGB model.
The colour representation can be
different, depending on the standards
of the primary colours produced by
different manufacturers.

In digital media colour costs
nothing to use, this is not the
case with print media. As a
result the new media designer
must resist the temptation to
use too many colours, as this
can often detract from an otherwise good design.

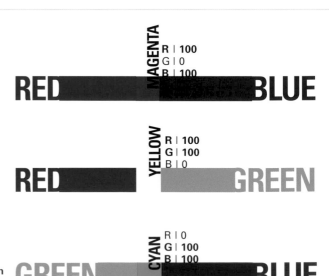

Additive colour system
Secondary colours I magenta, cyan, yellow

The subtractive colour system

We speak of subtractive colour mixing if dyes or pigments are mixed, for example in an ink duct.

This system operates with reflected light (absorption and reflection). The subtractive colour system is made up of the primary colours: cyan, magenta and yellow. If these colours all occur in equal intensity, this produces black. The secondary colours of the subtractive colour system are green, blue and red. Mixing the three primary colours does not produce a really deep black, therefore black (K) is added to the system, which is abbreviated as CMYK. It is used as a colour basis for printing.

Subtractive colour system
Primary colours I magenta, cyan, yellow

Subtractive colour system
Secondary colours I red, green, blue

2.01 Rules for the screen
Colour systems for the screen
Saturation, Brightness, Contrasts

Colours interact with one another. As a designer it is very important to know about colour contrast, saturation and brightness.

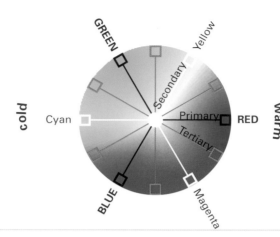

The sequence of colour hues can be conveniently presented as a colour wheel. Pairs of complementary colours, for example yellow and blue, are found on opposite sides of the wheel.

Saturation, Brightness and Contrast

If a colour is without hue, that is if the saturation is zero, then the result is achromatic (white, grey, or black). A pure colour, without any other colours added to it has the maximum saturation.

Each colour has its own brightness. Colour contrast plays an important role when it comes to the legibility of texts, particularly on the monitor screen. It is therefore important to select the colours carefully (**1.1**, **1.2**) because if the contrast is not sufficient it will be hard to tell what the message is (**1.3**, **1.4**). If there is too much contrast then there will be flickering, as in the case with complementary contrasts between colours on opposing sides of the colour wheel (**2.1**, **2.2**, **2.3**).

The effect of colours is always dependent on their setting. In different colour environments the same colour can have very different effects. Yellow, for example, combined with black (**3.1**) suggests danger (wasps), and attracts attention. Combined with green there is no tension, because the colours are very close on the colour wheel (**3.2**). Yellow and red (**3.3**), both »warm« colours, create a friendly, energetic impression.

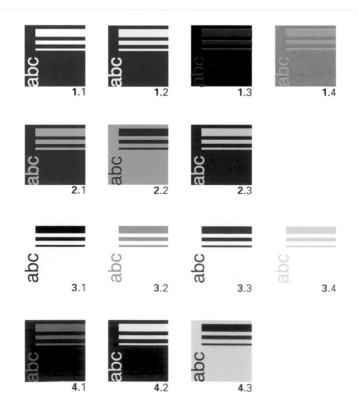

1.1–1.4 **Brightness contrasts**
2.1–2.3 **Complementary contrasts**
3.1–3.4 **Quality contrasts**
4.1–4.3 **Non-colour contrasts**

Striking colour contrasts should be avoided on information websites because they make reading text more difficult. But they can be very useful on start pages to grab visitors' attention.

Achromatic and achromatic-chromatic contrast (**4.1–4.3**) on the screen offers good options for presenting text in a way that is legible and easy on the eyes if the background is kept black or dark grey. However, there is a risk that the presentation may then seem drab and sombre.

One way to generate dramatic colour combinations is to use the temperature contrast (**5.1–5.6**). The colours should be chosen so as to avoid blooming and flickering. These undesirable effects are encountered in particular when colours have high saturation or brightness. If a coloured text is placed against a coloured background, then the graphic designer will have to increase the pitch to ensure that the result can be read without difficulty.

Colour-in-colour combinations (**7.1–7.3**) are well-suited as backgrounds for some elements such as logos, but not for texts because of the lack of contrast.

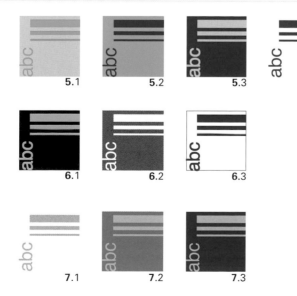

5.1–5.2 **warm and cold contrasts** I temperature contrasts
5.3–5.4 **warm and warm contrasts** I temperature contrasts
5.5–5.6 **cold and cold contrasts** I temperature contrasts
6.1–6.3 **achromatic and chromatic contrasts**
7.1–7.3 **combinations of colour tones**

2.02 **Rules for the screen**
Colours and their effect
Positive and negative associations

The choice of colours for the screen is a real challenge for the designer, because the colours are not only seen as colours in their own right, but are also seen within a specific cultural and perceptual context – a particular problem for international publications.

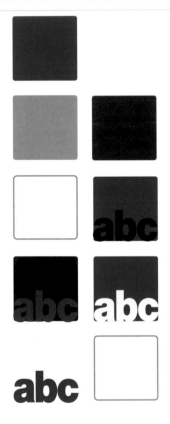

Colours and their effect

The screen background is usually the largest area of colour, so it should be selected with care. Every colour has its own character and it is important to consider how it will fit together with the colour of other design elements such as the typography or a logo.

The impression created by a colour is an important selection criterion. Red has a very emotive character and can be used just as well to symbolise aggression or revolution as it can for love and dynamism. A slight change of hue towards pink and the red can be reserved, tender and loving; a dark red can show demeanour and seriousness. Then there is the combination of colours: the quantity contrast describes the ratio of the amounts of colour used, the quality contrast the actual contrast between the colours themselves. A vivid red combined with black has a very deep

effect, but together with yellow it has a lively effect.

According to Goethe, it is possible to distinguish between passive and stimulating colours: yellow, orange, and red, for example, are active; blue, green, and violet are passive.

Whether a colour will be perceived positively or negatively will also depend on the mood, the subjective experience and the cultural background of the observer.

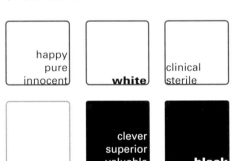

»...thus Heine the Proud carried a blue coat of arms,
which showed his cold soul and his pitiless heart;
Fasold and his brother Ecke bore a coat of arms with a red lion,
whose colour was an expression of their belligerence.«

Dietrich von Bern

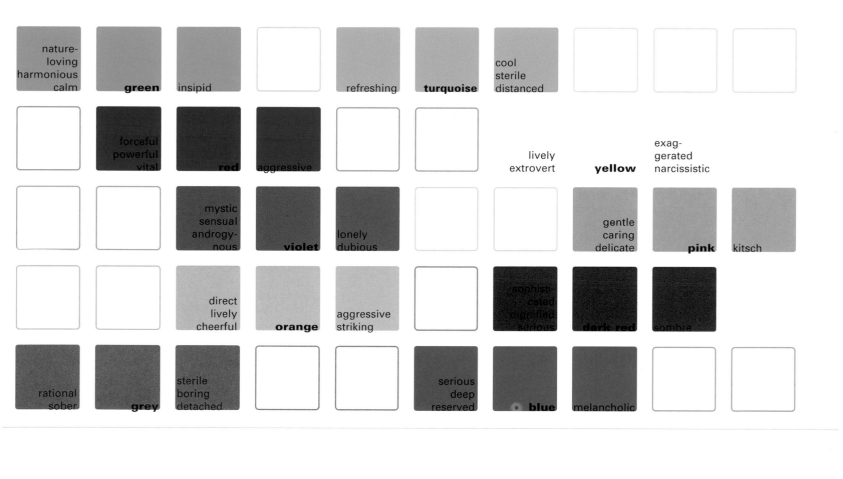

nature-loving harmonious calm	**green**	insipid		refreshing	**turquoise**	cool sterile distanced			
	forceful powerful vital	**red**	aggressive			lively extrovert	**yellow**	exaggerated narcissistic	
		mystic sensual androgynous	**violet**	lonely dubious			gentle caring delicate	**pink**	kitsch
		direct lively cheerful	**orange**	aggressive striking		sophisticated dignified serious	**dark red**	sombre	
rational sober	**grey**	sterile boring detached			serious deep reserved	**blue**	melancholic		

| europe usa purity cleanliness | **white** | asia india misfortune sadness | europe crucifixion death | **violet** | middle east prostitution | korea trust | **pink** | europe soft childish |

Colours have a different significance in different cultures. As a designer this is something you should take into account when selecting colours.

2.02 **Rules for the screen**
Colours and their effect
Colours for the screen

When selecting a colour for the screen it is
important to consider how much intensity
the viewer can take. Strong colours should
only be used on a home page or on pages
with little text.

An orange like that used by Veuve Clicquot
(1.1, 1.2) or a yellow used by the advertising
agency Scholz & Friends (2.1, 2.2) seems more
lively than the dark blue of DaimlerChrysler
(3.1, 3.2), which transmits a rational and serious
message in keeping with the product.

1.1

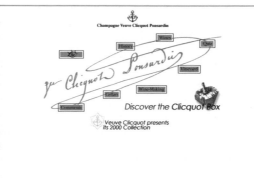

1.2

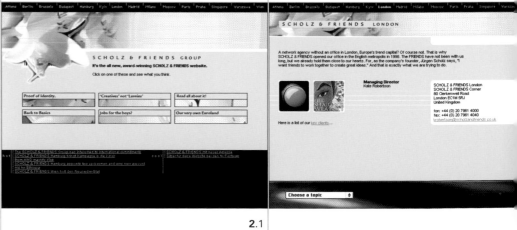

2.1

»By contrast with the generally held opinion, I would say
that colour has a far more secret and powerful strength;
it takes effect, so to speak, without our knowledge.«
Eugène Delacroix

4.1

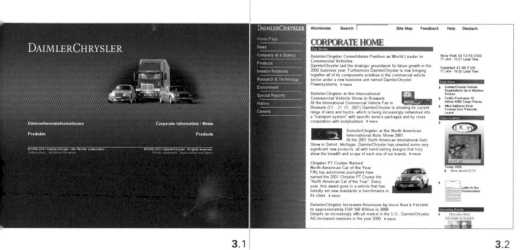

3.1

3.2

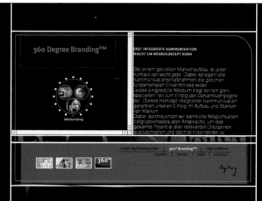

4.2

5.1

5.2

Although the websites of Jaguar (4.1)
and Ogilvy (4.2) both use black for their
background, the different quality contrasts
create completely different impressions.

Changing the background of the Porsche
Design home page (5.1, 5.2) from an
elegant black to a loud green transforms
the effect of the website. It loses all its
elegance and seems brash, superficial,
and hectic.

2.03 Rules for the screen
Choice of typefaces
Serifs, sans serifs and other typefaces

Typefaces have to be assessed individually for their legibility on screen. But as a general rule, serif typefaces are not as easy to read on screen as sans serifs.

Letters composed of:	Bembo	Bodoni	Garamond	Times
+ vertical lines	T	T	T	T
/ diagonal lines	A	A	A	A
○ curves	P	P	P	P

Serifs

Serif typefaces, which are used every day all over the world in newspapers (such as The Times), are not ideal for use on the screen where they tend to make reading more difficult, particularly for longer texts.

The small bases and slopes of the letters in serif types represent a problem for easy reading on screen. They become very ragged and create an impression of disorder. Another characteristic of serif types is the difference in line thickness. In some cases, for example with Bodoni, the very thin lines can lead to unfortunate effects.

If serif typefaces are used for screen presentations, it is important to ensure that the serifs and lines are not too thin, and that very small fonts are not used.

TANITH dates : foren : mixe : charts : texte : pics : links : shop

Web side

»Have you ever wondered why your monitor shows a stepped pattern? [...]
Why does a capital E, L or T look clean and tidy on the screen,
but a capital S, W or O look rather like amateur
Christmas tree decorations?
Why does a curved line on the computer look
as if the artist had a compulsive shake?
The reason is that only one bit per pixel was used for the display
on the computer. The result is the so-called staircase effect, also known
as aliasing, which would be completely unnecessary if hardware and software
manufacturers were to tackle the problem by using more computing power and
simply use more bits per pixel.«

Nicholas Negroponte

Futura	Gill Sans	Helvetica	Univers
T	T	T	T
A	A	A	A
P	P	P	P

Helvetica 56	Helvetica faux italic	Times italic	Times faux italic
T	T	T	T
A	A	A	A
P	P	P	P

Sans serifs

In contrast to the serif typefaces, sans serif types such as Gill Sans, Futura, or Univers have a uniform line thickness and make a much clearer impression. As the name implies, they have no serifs. The capital letter »T«, for example, consists only of straight lines, and will be completely free of any jagged steps. But there are problems with steps when it comes to the presenting of round letters, such as O, P, Q, etc.

Others

Italic typefaces (such as Helvetica 56) should be avoided on screen whenever possible. Even on paper, long texts in italics are tiring to read, but on screen all the diagonal lines develop the characteristic step-like patterns. Their use should be restricted to individual words.

The same applies to calligraphic typefaces, experimental typefaces and highlighting. These too should only be used sparingly, as eye-catchers for individual words or logos. Whether a typeface is appropriate for a given use has to be decided for each case separately.

Panama	Erikrighthand
TAP	TAP

Trixie Plain	Remedy Double
TAP	TAP

Helvetica Shadow	Times Shadow
TAP	TAP

Arial Outline	Times Outline
TAP	TAP

2.03 Rules for the screen
Choice of typefaces
Serifs and sans serifs

serifs

The new iBook gives you even more choices.
Your Life. To Go.

Your Life. To Go.

Serif typefaces are only partly suitable for use on screen.
The fine hairline strokes (serifs) are either ragged or
distorted – or they are not displayed at all. The same
applies to the frequent variations in the line thickness in
serif typefaces. These line thicknesses can quickly become
almost too thin for the resolution of the screen, especially
in small type sizes, so the line thickness in the display
may be different (depending on how each letter falls into
the pixel grid).
If it is unavoidable to use serif typefaces, e.g. for logos,
care must be taken to ensure that the type is large
enough.

.... to FABER-
CASTELL in the
Internet. I am pleased to
be able to use this
modern method to
present Germany's

FABER-CASTELL

sans serif

LAUNCH THE NAVIGATION

D:SPARA.TEN

LEFT INTERFERENCES 355
MENU ARCHIVES 209KB
GIVE ABOUT 237KB
A EMAIL
ACCESS
TO

D:SPARA.TEN
EXTEND YOUR BROWSER TO THE MAX
AND USE THE LEFT MENU TO NAVIGATE TROUGH THIS SITE

In comparison with the serif fonts, the grotesque fonts
are much clearer to read when used in displays.

RECHERCHEZ UNE POLICE DE CARACTÈRES PAR NOM

GO   RECHERCHE AVANCÉE

L'OUVRAGE DE RÉFÉRENCE

la typographie selon invalid.net

If italic styles, highlights or experimental fonts are used on screen, take care to ensure that the type size is large enough and that these fonts are only used for individual words or logos. Due to the extremely poor resolution, they should never be used for copy text.

//sorten muld

Sony Music

NYHEDER

Den længe ventede fortsættelse af Sorten Mulds unikke verden er nu frigivet.
10 stærke sange, der søger videre ud i mødet mellem den nordiske
balladetradition og et større batteri af elektronisk isenkram.

Vil du høre noget af den nye med Sorten Muld? - se PLADER under LYD

Vil du vide mere ? - se under INFO
Og hvad skriver de tœneanglme anmeldere ? - se UDKLIP under INFO

Eksklusiv koncerttour Efter 4 udsolgte forestillinger i Århus Festuge, i
samarbejde med MBT Danseteater, vil Sorten Muld Orchestra - på egen hånd
- besøge Danmarks 3-4 største byer i september og oktober:

Århus - Voxhall 23.09

//sorten muld

Buddha™ Graphix

??? Artwork

FonTDesigN

WebDesigN   MultiMedia

Art WiThout a Cause

Links   Kontakt

In some publications or screen presentations
legibility is not the prime concern – the typeface
is used instead as an illustration or an exciting
image.

Herausgegeben von
Alexander Branczyk
Heike Nehl
Sibylle Schlaich
Jürgen Siebert

Portraying Contemporary Type Designs

emotional_digital

ecv...

Établissement
d'enseignement
supérieur privé

77, rue du Cherche Midi
75006 Paris
Tél +01 42 22 21 33

580, avenue Mozart
13100 Aix en Provence
Tél 04 42 27 53 41 15

42, quai des Chartrons
33000 Bordeaux
Tél 05 56 52 90 52

graphisme
conception·multimédia
typographie·image
creation
illustration

digital

graphisme
conception·édition·multimédia
typographie·image
creation
illustration

2.03 Rules for the screen
Choice of typefaces
Type styles

Not all type styles are suitable for use on screen. Particularly italics and narrow and thin styles have to be set against a suitable background.

Line thickness | synonyms

2z
extrathin
ultralight
ultralight

3z
thin

4z
light

5z
normal
book
regular
roman

6z
medium
semibold

7z
bold

8z
extrabold
heavy

9z
black

Typefaces on the screen

With Internet screen display, there is a difference between text created as a graphic image and text saved as copy text. Two fonts can be used for copy text, depending on the browser configuration: Helvetica and Times for the Mac, and Arial and Times New Roman for the PC. These fonts can be either »normal« or »bold« in style. For better legibility on screen, the sans serif font at a size of 10–12 point is preferable. This constraint on the choice of font does not apply to graphics or to CD-ROMs. Fundamentally, all fonts and styles can be used here. However, you should bear a number of things in mind:

The effect of the background on the typeface plays a major role. The whiteness of the screen is brighter than paper because it is made up of light. This means that a font is always obscured somewhat by »blooming«, which makes the type appear thinner than it is. The effect of a font must therefore always be tested with different backgrounds, because the actual effect depends on the colour combinations.

Typefaces and styles, especially those which are less suitable for the screen, can be smoothed digitally so that they appear »cleaner« (1.1). The very bold and italic type styles should be spaced out slightly beforehand. Anti-aliasing should not be used with small type sizes (see pages 68–69).

not anti-aliased **not anti-aliased** **not anti-aliased**
anti-aliased **anti-aliased** **anti-aliased** 1.1

type
type *type* type type type *type* type
type type type type *type* type
type *type* type *type* type *type* type **type** type **type** **type** type

2.1

High contrast texts are registered before low-contrast texts, even if these are given a larger font size. In the example on the left this is supported by the use of a bolder style.

Letter spacing | synonyms

y2 extra expanded
extra extended

y3 expanded
extended

y5 normal
regular

y7 condensed
compressed
narrow

y9 extra condensed

Line slopes | synonyms

y5 normal
regular

y4/6/8 italic
oblique
slanted

		extra extended _2	extended _3	extended italic _4	normal _5	normal italic _6	condensed _7	condensed italic _8	extra condensed _9
ultralight	2_		Mmg	Mmg	Mmg	Mmg	Mmg	Mmg	
thin	3_		Mmg	Mmg	Mmg	Mmg	Mmg	Mmg	
light	4_		Mmg	Mmg	Mmg	Mmg	Mmg	Mmg	
normal	5_		Mmg	Mmg	Mmg	Mmg	Mmg	Mmg	
medium	6_		Mmg	Mmg	Mmg	Mmg	Mmg	Mmg	
bold	7_		Mmg	Mmg	Mmg	Mmg	Mmg	Mmg	
heavy	8_		Mmg	Mmg	Mmg	Mmg	Mmg	Mmg	
black	9_		Mmg	Mmg	Mmg	Mmg	Mmg	Mmg	

A type family differs in its various line thicknesses, line slopes and letter spacing: the type styles. To designate a member of a type family precisely, first the font name, then the line thickness, then the pitch and then the line slope is given, for example: Helvetica, medium, narrow and italic. The designations can differ widely depending on the type designer and manufacturer. For each font style there are a variety of synonyms. To shorten this list and standardise the details given, numbers are used for some fonts: the tens denote the line thickness, the units denote the line slope and letter spacing. The example shown above is Helvetica 68.

Not all font styles are suitable for the screen. Ultralight and light styles are not suitable for the screen because the lines are too thin for the pixels unless the type is used in very large type sizes. Italic styles and narrow letter spacing should also be avoided. Normal, expanded and bold type styles are very suitable. With bold type, the lines should not be too thick because this could make the letters run together. To ensure good legibility, the letter spacing should be wider, but this has the disadvantage of creating an ungainly impression.

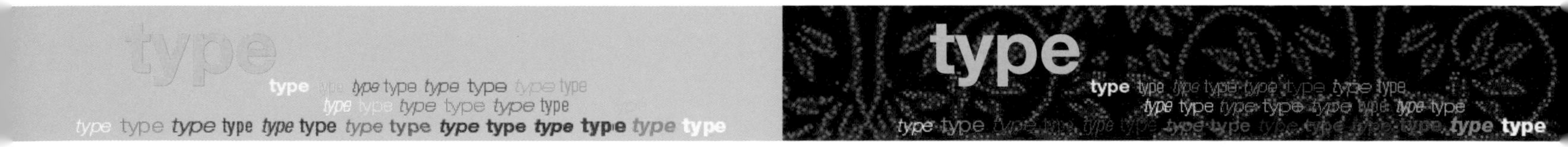

A patterned background requires a larger font size than a plain background. Make sure there is a clear colour contrast between the type and the background to ensure legibility (2.1).

2.04 Rules for the screen
Line length | text quantity
Strokes per line | Lines per column

The correct line length and appropriate text quantity for the screen have a positive effect on the ease with which the text will be read and understood.

1.1
The lines are too long for the screen
the eye loses the connection to the next line

| Univers | 10 | 20 | 30 | 38 |

Line length and text quantity

Not only is the choice of a suitable type size and font important, so is the correct line length as this also affects legibility of text on screen. For optimum legibility, columns on paper should only have up to ten words, or 35 to 55 keystrokes. On screen, however, the column width (or line length) should not be more than 35 keystrokes, even though the horizontal format of the screen actually seems to encourage long lines. Too many keystrokes per line must be avoided because otherwise there is a risk that the text, which is already of poor resolution, will be even more difficult to read.

This would be unattractive for the reader, as would lines that are too short and have either too much hyphenation or lines consisting of just a single word.

The text quantity should be reduced to the minimum in the interest of comprehension and legibility – ten to 25 lines per text block are ideal. Short text blocks can be distributed on the basis of the content without appearing disjointed. Here, a grid can be very useful. If it is essential for a text to be shown in full, the text can be sub-divided by using sub-headings, paragraphs, graphics or colour coding (adding colour on screen does not involve any extra cost, unlike print).

A good column width on paper.

The text in the example above on the left is very difficult to read because the lines are too long. The three short blocks in the example on the right are easier to read.

2.1–2.4
The best width for a column always depends on the letter spacing of the individual typeface. Times runs very narrow in comparison to screen fonts such as Verdana or New York, which were developed for optimum legibility on screen.

3.1
These line lengths are too short for good legibility of the text.

Verdana | 10 | 20 | 30 | 40 | 50 | 60 | 70 | 80 | 90

Not only the choice of a suitable type size and font is important: the choice of the correct line length also has a positive effect on the legibility of texts on screen.

Monaco | 10 | 20 | 30 | 35

Verdana | 10 | 20 | 30 | 35

Helvetica | 10 | 20 | 30 | 35

Times | 10 | 20 | 30 | 35

New York | 10 | 19

Not only is the choice of a suitable type size and font important, so is the correct line length as this also affects legibility of text on screen.

Not only is the choice of a suitable type size and font important, so is the correct line length as this also affects legibility of text on screen.

Not only is the choice of a suitable type size and font important, so is the correct line length as this also affects legibility of text on screen.

Not only is the choice of a suitable type size and font important, so is the correct line length as this also affects legibility of text on screen.

Not only is the choice of a suitable type size and font important, so is the correct line length as this also affects legibility of text on screen.

2.05

Rules for the screen
Line spacing I word spacing
Increasing the dimensions

Options such as increased line spacing can make
text much easier to read on monitor screens.

The line spacing on screen should be wider than on paper,
which is easily legible with 120% (automatic setting).

Paper: type size 14 pt I line spacing 120% (automatic setting) = 16.8 pt
Screen: type size 14 pt I line spacing 130% = 18.2 pt

130% I Frutiger I 14 pt

Line spacing and word spacing

Poor display of type on screen does not
offer a particularly great incentive for
reading. In your design you should try
and use features which make the text
easier to read. The selection of the line
spacing is an important criterion for the
overall impression and the incentive to
read a text. If the line spacing is too
narrow, the reader will be reluctant to
read the text because it appears too
dense and compact. If we assume that
35 characters per inch line are ideal to
read on screen, the line spacing should
be 130–150% of the solid type (3.1). The
longer the line is, the greater the line
spacing that is needed for the text. Wide
and thin type styles need a greater line
gap, whereas narrow and bold styles
need less.

If the line spacing is too wide, the gaps
dominate the visual impression instead
of the text, and the eye finds it difficult
to connect with the next line.

The letter spacing for texts should be
wider by five to ten units. That especially
applies to bold styles, because otherwise
the letters may run together or merge in
small sizes, which means that letters
may be misread (1.1, 2.1).

ol
rn
d
2.1

Helvetica 55 with standard character spacing
Helvetica 55 with character spacing set to plus 5

Helvetica 75 with standard character spacing
Helvetica 75 with character spacing set to plus 5
Helvetica 75 with character spacing set to plus 10

Helvetica 75 I 8 pt I +10
Helvetica 75 I 14 pt I +5
Helvetica 75 I 14 pt I +10

1.1 The bolder the type style, the greater the letter spacing.
The larger the type size, the smaller the letter spacing.

Headline

It wasn´t so very long ago that the term »anarchy« struck terror into the soul of the middle classes: fantasies were abound of a society without control, and of law and order, political authority and accepted structures being swept away. Today in the Internet age the term »anarchy« takes on a different meaning, radiating an aura of something positive, that which is desired. The Internet, a grass-roots evolution, a podium for free speech and an engine of democracy, stands opposed to existing hierarchies. It is against centralisation, capital, authority, structures and any game plan order.

If authority is abandoned then the stage is set for the illusion of self-control to take over, which aspires to no particular goal. This lawlessness not only spawns a mass of information lacking any specific aims, but also intolerable lawlessness in terms of the way the information is supplied and its aesthetic quality.

Headline

It wasn´t so very long ago that the term »anarchy« struck terror into the soul of the middle classes: fantasies were abound of a society without control, and of law and order, politic authority and accepted structures being swept away. Today in the Inter net age the term »anarchy« takes on different meaning, radiating an aura of something positive, that which is desired. The Internet, a grass-roots evolution, a podium for free speech and an engine of demo-cracy, stands opposed to existing hierarchies. It is against centralisation, capital, authority, structures and any game plan order.

120%

Headline

If authority is abandoned then the stac is set for the illusion of selfcontrol to ta over, which aspires to no particular goa This lawlessness not only spawns a mas of information lacking any specific aim but also in-tolerable lawlessness in term of the way the information is supplied and its aesthetic quality. Paradoxically, instead of enjoying a freedom newly won, we experience the very lack of it, because the way the information is coded is a many-layered maze in the middle of which the recipient becomes lost.

100%

3.1
The column above is set in 14 pt Frutiger.
The letter spacing is +5, the line spacing is 130% so that the text is easy to read on screen.

3.2
The column above is set in 14 pt Frutiger.
The letter spacing and the line spacing (120%) of the upper text are standard.
The bottom text is spaced by -5 units, the line spacing is 100%.
Neither of the examples in the column above is as good to read as the spaced out example in 3.1.

2.05 Rules for the screen
Line spacing | word spacing
Increasing the dimensions

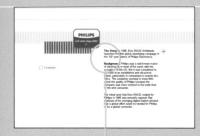

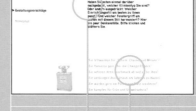

The text on advertising agency Euro
RSCG's website has been well
structured into paragraphs, and the
quantity is not too great so it can be
grasped at a glance. The line length
is adjusted to the disadvantages of the
screen.

The Story: In 1998, Euro RSCG Worldwide
launched the first global advertising campaign in
the 107-year history of Philips Electronics.

The website of the FSB company also works well
with brief paragraphs of text. The texts are arranged on
different reading levels so that the viewer can easily
distinguish and choose between the main information
and supplementary information.
For the main information the type is black, while
supplementary information is displayed in grey type.

The website of the furniture manufacturer Wilkhahn is clearly structured: The left column of text, which is easy to follow because of the combination of a good type size and a line length that is easy to read, contains an introduction. The reader can then use the right hand column to call up more detailed information.

The text blocks on the Audi website are narrow, which makes for greater legibility and easy comprehension of the content. The short texts have been split up into individual blocks which are distributed around the website.
The FSB also differentiates texts on a hierarchical principle: less important sections are in narrower type styles than the more important sections, which appear bolder.

2.05 **Rules for the screen**
Line spacing | word spacing
Increasing the dimensions

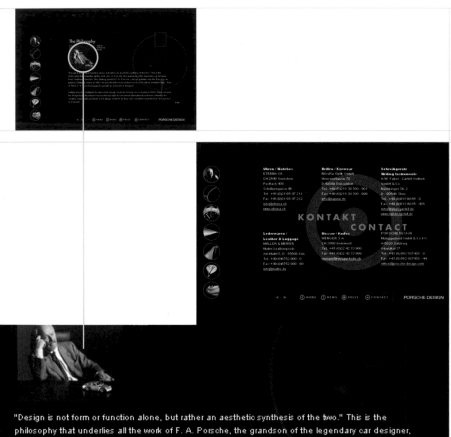

If a text is very long and the website cannot be scrolled, the width of the screen can be exploited by using various design principles – such as the careful selection of typefaces and font sizes, the use of leading, and the colour contrast between the text and the background. The lines of text in the Porsche Design website, for example, are very long for a website. But with the generous line spacing and a large type size, the text can still be read easily.

Plumb design: a good and clearly structured two-column distribution of space. The left column contains the main information, the right in smaller, coloured type contains the links to the main information.

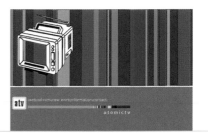

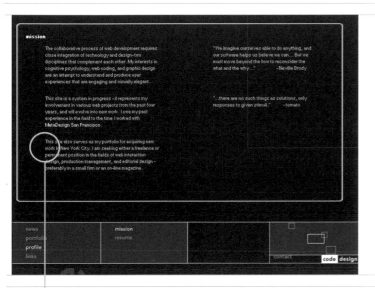

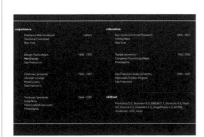

A very clearly structured website from Code Design which does not appear boring. The strict two column layout is given a slight edge by the visual emphasis given to the sub-headings.

If the text is too long to be contained in a site, it can be scrolled as in the ATV website. The line length does not need to be completely full.

2.06 **Rules for the screen**
Type size
Legibility on the monitor screen

A font size of at least 10 pt should be used for text on screen in order to make sure that it can be read easily.

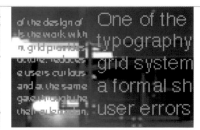
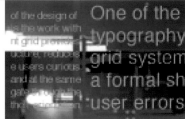

| 12 pt, not anti-aliased | 8 pt and 14 pt, not anti-aliased | 8 pt and 14 pt, anti-aliased |

Type sizes

The display of type on screen is considerably inferior to printed paper. Type sizes that are pleasant to read on paper cannot necessarily be transferred to the screen because of the poor resolution of computer monitors. Fonts in very small sizes, which may be quite legible on printed paper, can often hardly be seen on screen. Type sizes below 10 pt should therefore not be used on screen under any circumstances. The size of text on screen should be at least 10 pt, or even better, 11 pt to 14 pt. The corresponding heading should be between 14 pt and 20 pt. In fact, every font should be considered on its own merits: Serif typefaces should be

displayed in larger sizes than the more advisable sans serif fonts. It is advisable to test the fonts in different sizes and styles on different backgrounds: the larger the typeface, the more pixels are available and the clearer the display will be. Pixels are the dots on the computer monitor which, because of their modular character, can display almost anything. Their disadvantage is that they have a square structure, and this can create a jagged edge in curves and diagonals. If many pixels are available to display a diagonal, the individual »steps« will be finer.

Times | 8 pt   Univers | 8 pt   Frutiger | 8 pt

Times | 10 pt   Univers | 10 pt   Frutiger | 10 pt

Times | 12 pt   Univers | 12 pt   Frutiger | 12 pt

Times | 14 pt   Univers | 14 pt   Frutiger | 14 pt

anti-aliased   Times | 14 pt   **Univers | 14 pt**   **Frutiger | 14 pt**

Times | 20 pt   Univers | 20 pt   Frutiger | 20 pt

une des portes
NORMAL

8 pt and 14 pt, anti-aliased

If a typeface is difficult to read on a monitor screen then a larger font size must be used. This applies in particular if there is low contrast between text and background, or if »fractured« or experimental typefaces are used.

Smoothing of fonts

To transform a heavily pixel-based type display into clearly legible text, the steps can be artificially »smoothed«. Steps in curves and diagonals are filled in with intermediate colour shades, which make the resolution of the type appear finer. The type becomes a graphic image and appears in the font and layout it was typeset in.

Anti-aliasing should not be used with small type sizes.

not anti-aliased

anti-aliased   Univers 75 | 9 pt

not anti-aliased

anti-aliased   Univers 75 | 16 pt

Verdana | 8 pt

Verdana | 10 pt

Verdana | 12 pt

Verdana | 14 pt

Verdana | 14 pt   anti-aliased

Verdana | 20 pt

Anti-aliasing should only be used with bigger type sizes.

3.0 grids for the screen

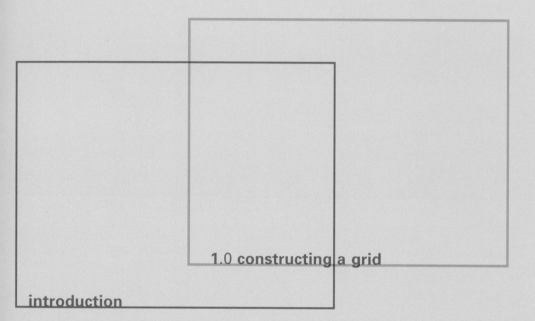

introduction

1.0 constructing a grid

basics:
typography & colour

2.0 rules for the screen

from print to screen

4.0 transfer of grids

3.0 grids for the screen

3.01 consequences for grid design | 072
3.02 programming languages | 076
3.03 flow charts – how to structure
     a concept | 078
3.04 structures for the screen | 084
3.05 distribution on a screen | 094
3.06 layout elements | 096
3.07 innovative grid solutions | 098
3.08 dos and don'ts | 114
3.09 front pages | 122
3.10 banners | 126
3.11 cd-roms | 128
3.12 mini-screens | 132

3.01 **Grids for the screen**
Consequences for grid design
Differences between print and screen

When you design digital screen presentations it is
not only important to take into account the specific
properties offered by the media – like animation,
interaction, and the flexibility of the presentations in
contrast to the permanence of print media – elements
which are also used in printed matter must be
adapted for use on screen. For example, the low
resolution of the screen and its landscape format
make it necessary to have a number of narrow
columns so that the text is easier to read. The freely
available colours must be used with care, and clear
navigation and orientation are very important so that
users are not to get lost in a maze of alternatives.
A well-planned grid system can help users find their
way around by making it easier to identify the
elements and functions.

1.1 **Front page**

Differences between print and screen

When setting up websites, there are
some rules from printing that remain
unchanged. But there are numerous
special aspects to be taken into account
that are crucial for good screen design.

One obvious point that is often overlooked is that print is usually presented
in a portrait format, but screen presentations have to be in a landscape
format. This has consequences for the
arrangement of grid elements on screen,
as well as for column widths and
lengths, positioning of illustrations and
other key elements.

Then there are the specialities offered
by the medium, such as animations,
moving text, or navigational elements.
When you are holding a book in your
hands it is possible to see and feel
whether you are at the beginning or end.
With screen interfaces, the users often
have no idea where they are, or how
they get from one page to another.
So the screen designer should pay
particular attention to the logistics
and visual hierarchies.

In the case of web design, there is one
problem that is not encountered in print
media, or video and CD publications,
namely HTML (Hypertext Mark-up
Language). This is the system for marking a text so that it can be published
on the World Wide Web. It speeds up
the exchange of documents, but with
the drawback that it is not possible to
specify the exact appearance of a page
for all possible recipients. However, a
well-thought out grid system can help
to reduce the negative effects, like a lack
of orientation and getting lost, to an
acceptable level.

The same uncertainties exist for the
presentation of colours. There can be
considerable differences between what
is seen by users of different computer
systems, and the individual settings of
each monitor (e.g. the brightness, or
colour balance) also have an effect.

The difference between the subtractive
colour system of printing and the
additive system of screen images

The website of the business consulting company Kleimann & Partner, an HTML document, manages with fewer colours.

Following pages 1.2, 1.3

means that colours cannot be simply transferred on to the screen. »Exactly« soon becomes »more or less«, and perfectionists have to bring a degree of tolerance with them if they want to work with new media.

One striking advantage that new media offers over traditional print media is that any number of colours can be used at no extra cost. But although this sounds very tempting it needs to be handled with care (1.1–1.3). The same rule applies for typography, added features and animations: use as much as necessary rather than as much as possible.

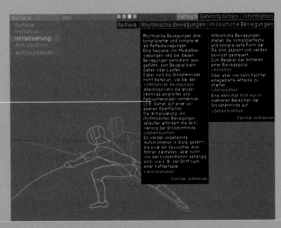

The landscape format means that the texts must be spread over a number of narrow columns, such as here on a CD-ROM about speed. The designer should avoid the use of broad columns, because these are difficult to read on screen.

The design of orientation and the clarity of navigation are extremely important for a digital presentation, where the sequences can be determined interactively. In contrast to print publications, which have a given linear sequence, pagination does not help much at all.

3.01   Grids for the screen
Consequences for grid design
Extended grids

Due to the differences in hardware and software between users, the »classical« grid from the world of printing has to be extended to include additional parameters in order to provide visual and functional continuity.

 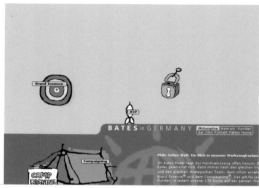

Aesthetic grid
The unusual style of the Bates' website generates a feeling of continuity and makes it readily identifiable.

Extended grid

The »classical« pre-defined grid is no longer appropriate for the design of a website, since things that can be precisely defined on paper often simply become approximations on the web. This is because users have different software, different browser configurations, different versions of operating systems, not to mention different hardware, with different monitor screen sizes and different colour cards. When print products are distributed, their final appearance has already been determined, and will only change through ageing or poor storage, but with a website the transmitted dataset is subject to subsequent interpretation, and can be presented in very different ways to the recipient depending on a variety of factors. The scope for fine detail that is offered by precise typography or when determining print colours, is severely restricted on the Internet, and because it is only possible to give recommendations, the grid concept has to be extended to include additional parameters. The modular units relate to an abstract grid rather than to some idea of mathematical precision.

A grid includes everything associated with the set of rules determining the continuity, the identification, and the orientation.

Function and hierarchy grid
Standard arrangement and coding of functional elements such as navigation bars and the orientation guides.

Colour grid
Definition of functions and areas by use of colour.

Sound grid
Definition of interactions by sound.

Movement and time grids
Action and speed of moving objects.

Quotation grid
Fixed images with text and illustration, which cannot be altered by user settings.

Aesthetic grid
The unchanging character of presentation of a website.

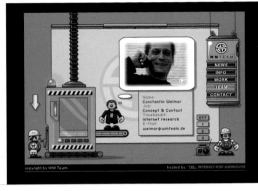

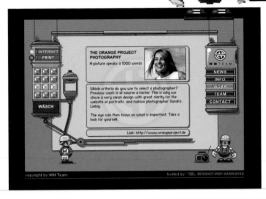

Movement and time grids

The movements of the small figures draws attention to the interactive areas and to information.

When the orange area containing the information opens, it is centred on a black frame, so that the presentation is not dependent on the size of the monitor screen.

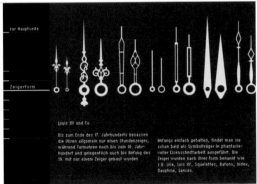

Function and hierarchy grid

The navigation bar of the CD-ROM »dial-plate« is always on the left and attention is drawn to it by the colour-coding against the other black-white-grey areas.

Colour grid | Sound grid

Definition of areas by colour changes and sound feedback. If an object is successfully selected, the user receives feedback – the object changes colour and a sound is heard.

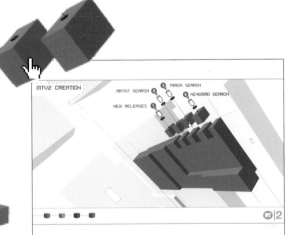

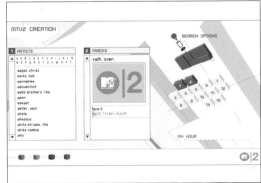

Useful Information

o **DEAR PASSENGER:**
o **CONDITIONS OF CONTRACT**

100%

Quotation grid

The appearance of a website depends very much on the user settings.
For the website of Aeroflot the settings for »text« were changed.
The buttons of the navigation bar and the logo were not affected by the settings because they are provided as graphics.

Static pages (HTML) have the advantage that they can be downloaded quickly. Dynamic pages (Flash, D-HTML) can be more entertaining, with the inclusion of animations, but a page takes longer to appear on screen than an HTML-page would. The choice of programming language depends on what the website is needed for.

HTML

HTML (Hyper Text Mark-up Language)
HTML is a mark-up language for the editing of websites. Its formatting tags specify the presentation of text, graphic elements and images: HTML is a text-description and layout language for web information and not a programming language as such. HTML is mainly used for websites when a short loading time is important and quick access to information has priority over entertainment value. Pages in search engines, timetables, flight information for airlines, booking forms for car hire services, as well as on-line newspapers are all usually produced using HTML: typical applications containing considerable amounts of information.

HTML pages are static, that is without moving elements. The information changes within frames, and the user goes through the website from page to page.

D-HTML

D-HTML (Dynamic HTML)
D-HTML is a term used for systems offering the options that are provided by the combination of languages such as CSS, HTML and Java-script. Depending on the actions of the user, D-HTML allows changes to be made to the presentation by the web browser. For example, individual parts of a page or specific elements can be switched on or off, or can be held in place when the page is being scrolled. In contrast to HTML it is also possible to include windows that can be opened and closed.
Using the layer technique of D-HTML, elements can be faded out or superimposed, the dynamics will depend on the user activity. The data is built up without the user noticing anything.

Moveable window which can optionally be closed down.

Moving element.

Flash

Flash
Flash is a software which can be used to generate animations. Effects which are impossible with HTML present no problems for Flash. These include movement and also the integration of sound. A further special feature is the adaptation of Flash-films to the monitor size by means of vector graphics. Flash can be linked to HTML pages.

HTML only gives a recommendation for the font that can be used. However, the browser can be forced to use a system font.

PURCHASING TICKETS
Booking tickets
Reserving tickets

The text is not anti-aliased...

...except with inserted graphics.

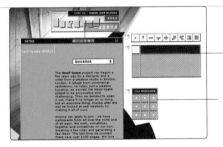

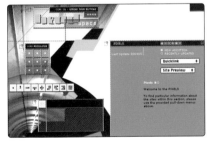

Pop-ups as moveable windows, or pull-down menus are elements which help to overcome the limitations of HTML.

Flash or D-HTML
Flash is frequently used by designers, as it was developed specially with web design in mind. D-HTML is more often used by programmers who come from the HTML world, the core of the web. D-HTML is a further development of HTML, which was developed in the early 1990s, when web design was still only of relatively minor importance. With Flash, which is not an industrial standard, the user needs an additional plug-in, and the site must not exceed a certain size. In addition the Flash sites are not picked up by search engines, so an HTML file has to be provided for the server for this purpose. The problem with D-HTML is that the various browser versions only support D-HTML in part, and then in different ways, so that the same D-HTML code can lead to different responses on different browsers.

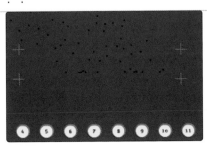

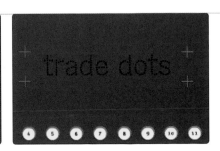

Flash animation with background sound.

3.03 **Grids for the screen**
Flow charts – How to structure a concept
The ladder diagram

Using flow charts (miniatures of the sequences and the distribution) it is possible to get an overview of text and pictures for each page. This can be a big help when it comes to determining the grid. The ladder diagram is a linear sequence showing the user the procedure for obtaining an answer to a specific request.

Flow charts

Before the screen designer designs the sequence of a website, he should make a sketch of the structure of the screen and the content. This structure is presented in the form of flow charts – thumbnail miniatures which illustrate the sequence, the links and the space for the volume of information. The links between screens are indicated by directional arrows. This enables any incorrect links to be discovered at an early stage.

Fundamentally, a distinction can be made between three basic models: the ladder diagram, the tree diagram and the network diagram. Which of these models is most appropriate depends on the requirements and functions of the website. Before the screen designer decides on a model, the target group must be determined and the content and function of the website must be defined. It is important to determine whether the website is directed at experienced or inexperienced users, whether the information should be provided in a guided structure or whether the user should be able to choose it freely.

The screen designer can use flow charts to develop a rough grid system and to estimate how the necessary information, such as text and images, can be distributed on the screen, how the pages should be linked and how many pages are needed. Finely tuned flow charts can be used to define and review the positioning of navigation elements, logos, menu bars, type areas and other recurring elements.

The planned overall impression, or any existing corporate design principles for a website or a CD-ROM presentation, can be checked at a glance on the flow charts.

By producing flow charts the screen designer can keep track of the quantity of contents and its distribution over the various pages. The pages with the least and the most contents form the basis for the organisation system of the elements – a grid.

Home page

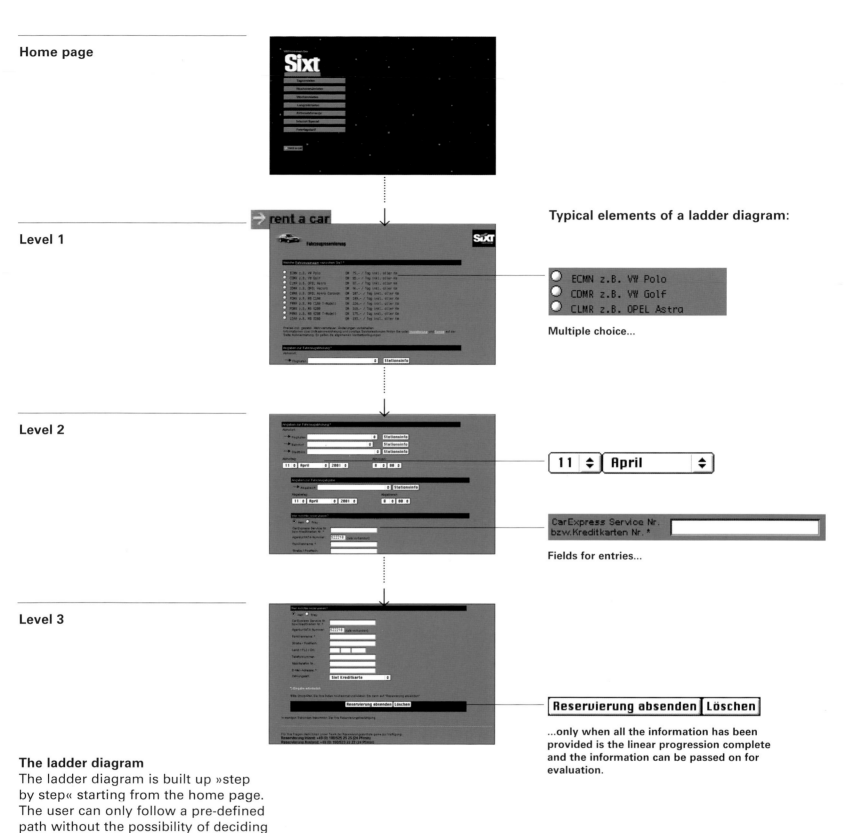

Level 1

→ rent a car

Typical elements of a ladder diagram:

Multiple choice...

Level 2

Fields for entries...

Level 3

...only when all the information has been provided is the linear progression complete and the information can be passed on for evaluation.

The ladder diagram

The ladder diagram is built up »step by step« starting from the home page. The user can only follow a pre-defined path without the possibility of deciding freely which information he wants to call up. But this inflexible navigation principle makes sense if the author of a website or CD-ROM wishes to guide the user through the information in a linear manner, for example in educational programs: the user can then only move on to the next lesson when he has successfully completed the present lesson. It is also appropriate when personal data are required for e-commerce – the example shows a form for a car hire company.

3.03 Grids for the screen
Flow charts – How to structure a concept
The tree diagram

The tree diagram is used when the information is
distributed hierarchically with main and secondary
branches.

Home page

Helpful elements of a tree diagram for orientation and navigation:

Level 1

The main menu, showing all the
key contents on offer.

Level 2

>>

The topics of the sub-menus are blown-up
as a background and as an orientation aid...

Clear symbols are also provided for
navigation on a third level.

...and it is marked with a symbol that the user
is already familiar with from the main menu.

Level 3

> START UPS
> HONORARBEISPIELE

< ZURÜCK

The number of symbols/nuts indicates
the depth of the information.

The user can jump between theory (> start ups)
and examples for the menu item (> fee examples),
or can navigate back to the previous page (< back).

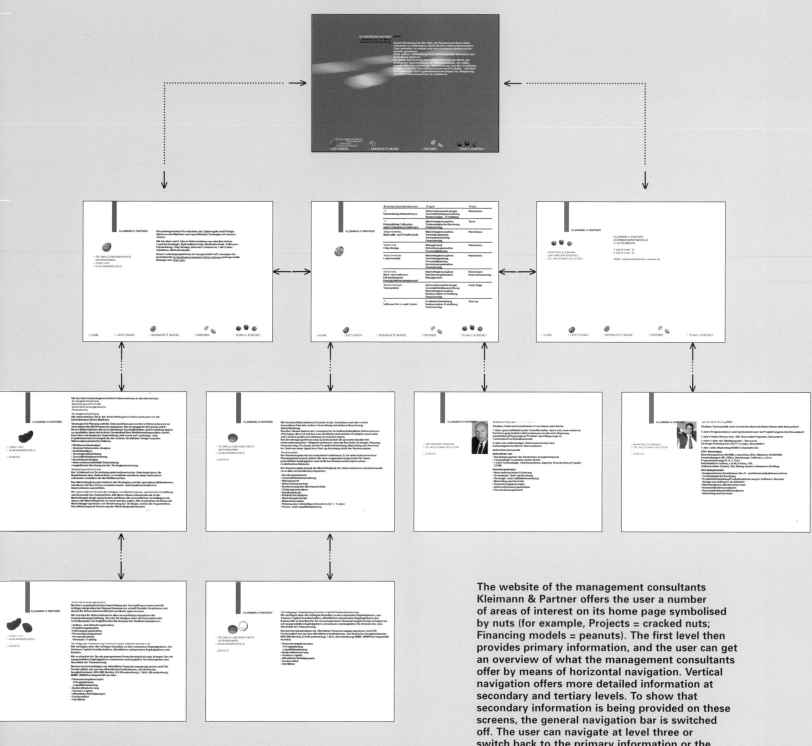

The website of the management consultants Kleimann & Partner offers the user a number of areas of interest on its home page symbolised by nuts (for example, Projects = cracked nuts; Financing models = peanuts). The first level then provides primary information, and the user can get an overview of what the management consultants offer by means of horizontal navigation. Vertical navigation offers more detailed information at secondary and tertiary levels. To show that secondary information is being provided on these screens, the general navigation bar is switched off. The user can navigate at level three or switch back to the primary information or the starting page. At level three a nut is added in the illustration field to assist orientation.

The tree diagram

Starting with the main menu (Level 1), this model branches out to various sub-menus. The model is used when secondary information, for example explanations, is added to primary information, or when information is provided with a hierarchical structure, with main topics and sub-topics. The problem with this model lies in the clear orientation of the options open to the user. There should either be only a limited number of links to secondary information or the navigation must be made very unambiguous.

3.03 Grids for the screen
Flow charts – How to structure a concept
The network diagram

The network diagram is the most open of all the
diagrams, because it offers the user the opportunity
to move directly from one page to any other.

Home page

Helpful elements of a network diagram for orientation and navigation:

Level 1

Transparent navigation and ease of orientation are
even more important with a network diagram than
with the other diagram models:

...and good navigation
between the sub-topics.

PRINZIPIELLES

...the main topic,

...a clear division into sub-topics,

Level 2

menü

Prinzipielles
Essentielles
Persönliches
Gelerntes
Geleistetes
Überzeugendes
Frisches
Lustvolles

menü

The menu appears on every page so that it is
possible to move on directly to any other page.
In this case it is closed to save space and...

...opens as soon as the user clicks on it.

Using a flow chart makes it
possible to gain an overview
of the navigation, and check the
logic of the overall structure of
the grid.

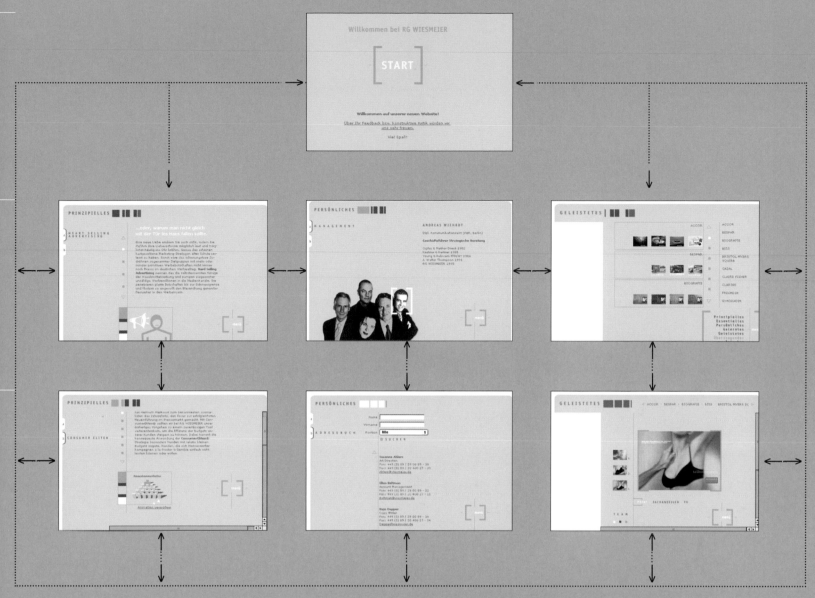

The Internet presentation of the advertising agency RG Wiesmeier is structured so as to allow the user to navigate freely from one page to another.

The network diagram
This model allows the user to navigate independently through the website. The advantage of this system is that information can be accessed directly and quickly. The disadvantage is that it is possible to lose all orientation, and this can be disconcerting for inexperienced users. Therefore when designing such systems, attention should be paid to clear navigation aids.

3.04 **Grids for the screen**
Structures for the screen
Grid sub-divisions

Functional elements that can always be found in
the same position on a grid help users to explore
freely without having to worry about losing track of
where they are.

1.1   1.2

Structures for the screen

Functional stability, rhythm and
uniformity are important factors that
help to ensure that a web page can be
understood. Speed of use is increased
if the functional elements are always
located in the same place.
Functionality and ease of navigation
can be improved if the designer adopts
the same grid system throughout. This
means that navigation fields, texts and
images can always be found in the
same fixed positions.
The effort that goes into developing
such a grid is well worth it. With this
backbone for the graphics, elements
can be placed much more efficiently
during the development, and the
users of the website benefit from
the improved orientation.
An ordered and logical set-up generates
its own visual identity. As a result, pages
added at a later date can easily be set
up so they fit in well with the existing
pages. It is not necessary to develop

a new basic layout for each new entry.
The grid should not be oriented on
the home page, but on the page with
the most text, illustrations, and the
most extensive navigation, and the
page with the least text, images and
navigation. Though it is tempting to
start with the home page, this can, in
fact, be produced easily once the
problems for the other pages have
been solved.

Proportions play an important role
when it comes to distributing the
functional elements on a web page
(**1.1**, **1.2**).

The proportions of the standard format
of 640 pixels (width) x 480 pixels (height)
gives a ratio of 4 : 3 (1.333).

This landscape format is particularly
good for a varied sub-division in grid
cells, because the elements can be
arranged in several columns.

2.1

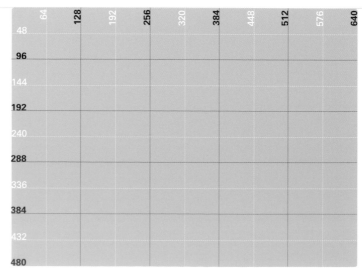

2.2

An impressive presentation is best achieved by choosing an asymmetrical array of functional elements in the grid (1.1, 1.2). Too much symmetry can seem clumsy, inflexible and boring.

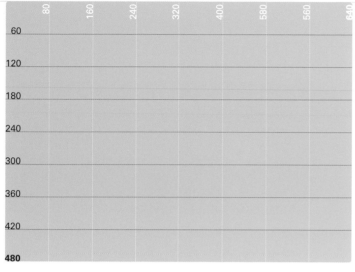

2.3

2.4

As shown in figure 2.4, a grid need not always consist of the same cells. The more detailed a grid, the more variable it can be.

Elements of a web page
Text field
Image field
Navigation field
Film field

Screen formats | in pixels
640 x 480
800 x 600
1024 x 768

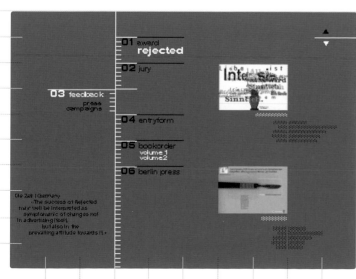

2.2.1

The figures 2.1 to 2.4 show possible sub-divisions of the standard format of 640 x 480 pixels.

This is the format usually used for multimedia CDs. The advantage is that it can be displayed well on smaller screens (14″ and 15″), and is also suitable for printing.

3.04 Grids for the screen
Structures for the screen
Navigation bar positioned to the left

In order to determine the grid for a website, it is best to position the »functional elements« first, for example the navigation bar. The remaining space is then freely available for other purposes.

It is very common to place the navigation bar on the left. People are accustomed to reading from left to right, but another advantage is that it makes sure that none of the navigation bar will get cut off if it is viewed on a smaller screen.

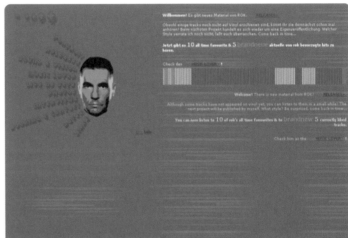

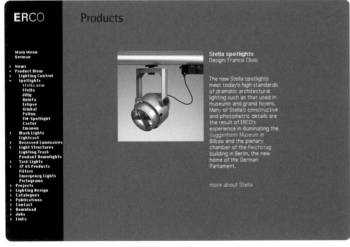

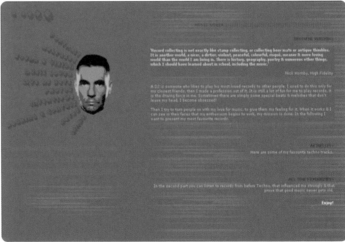

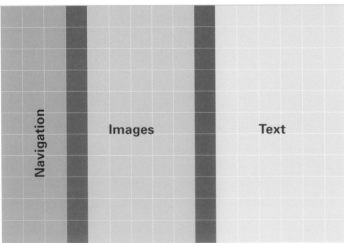

1.0

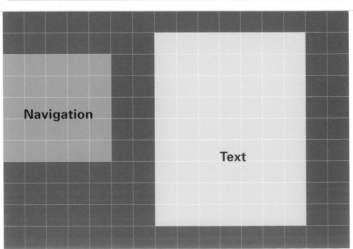

2.0

When creating a website, it is best to start with the navigation. The remaining space is then available for text and pictures.

From left to right:
The navigation bar is positioned to the left. This corresponds to most people's reading habits, but given that users will be using all sorts of monitors, it also ensures that no items are off-screen.
If the intention is to irritate the user, then elements can be placed bottom right, for example, but then they should be animated in order to attract attention to them in this unexpected position.

»Everything should be as simple as possible – but no simpler.«
Albert Einstein

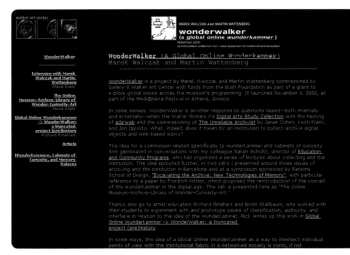

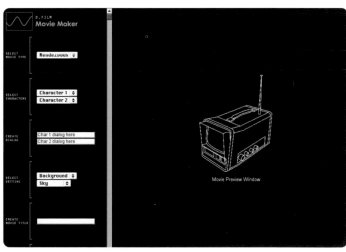

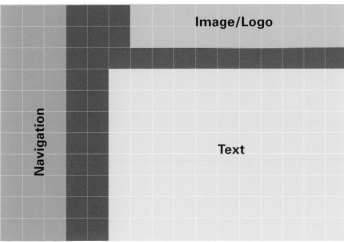

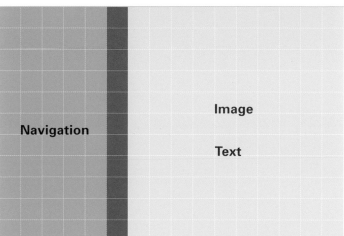

3.0

4.0

Navigation bar positioned horizontally at the bottom (left-hand page)
Navigation bar positioned horizontally and vertically (right-hand page)

Having the navigation bar running along the bottom of the screen leaves a lot of space for pictures and text, but it may be overlooked if it is not clear enough so care should be taken here. The navigation points should also be kept as brief as possible so that the page does not seem bottom-heavy. It is not a good idea to have in excess of two navigation bars per page, because they can easily become more of a hindrance than a help.

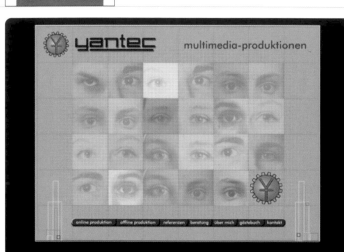

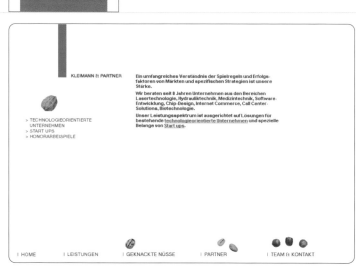

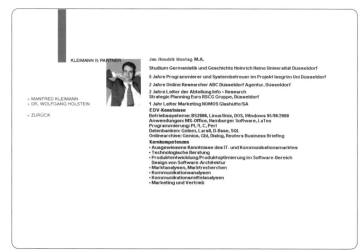

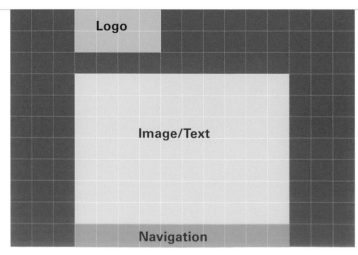

5.0

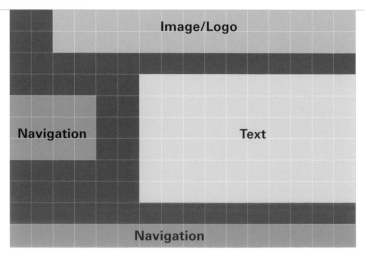

6.0

T
Too many navigation bars can make the overall structure appear restless, which has an irritating effect on the visual guidance. Therefore, there should be no more than two bars.

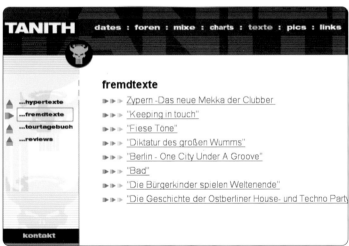

A web page normally consists of the basic elements such as a text field, image field and navigation field, and possibly also a film field.

The navigation field represents a list of contents, showing the various possibilities on offer, and is best located on the left side of the screen (**1**.0, **2**.0, **3**.0, **4**.0, **7**.0). This layout corresponds to the expectations of users in the western hemisphere, who read from left to right. First the structural information will receive attention and then the details. Another good reason for locating the navigation field on the left is that users will be looking at the page on monitors of varying shapes and sizes. If a page has been defined with a width of 800 pixels, then on a monitor with only 640 pixel resolution the right side of the page will not be visible. It may be cut off completely, or require a horizontal scroll before it appears.

The navigation bar can also be situated horizontally across the page if the information content consists mainly of pictures rather than text (**7**.0, **8**.0, **9**.0, **10**.0). Here there is the danger that it will come into conflict with the navigation bar of the browser.

The remaining space on the web page is the »net space« for all further information such as text, images, or film.

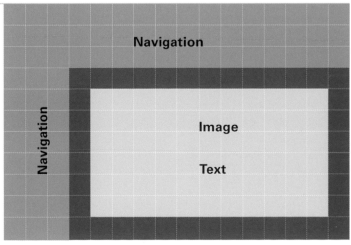

7.0

3.04 Grids for the screen
Structures for the screen
Navigation bar positioned horizontally in the middle

A central horizontal navigation bar can be an interesting option if the information content of a page contains more pictures than text, or only has short texts.

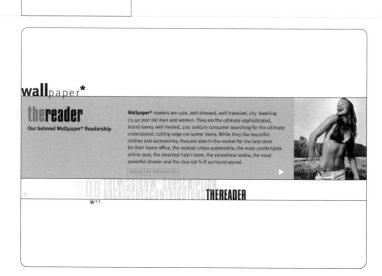

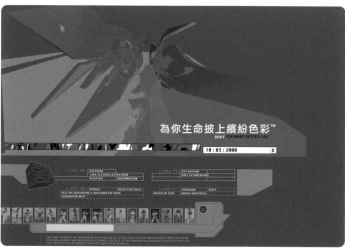

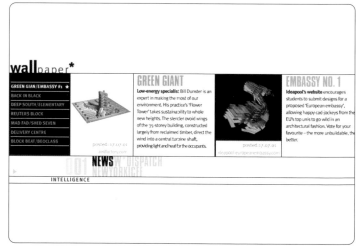

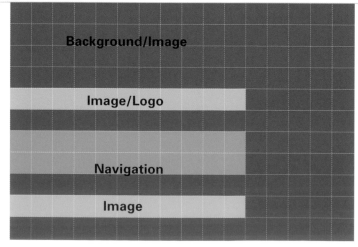

Background/Image

Image/Logo

Navigation

Image

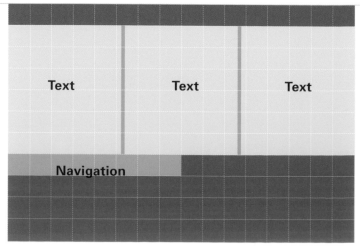

Text   **Text**   **Text**

Navigation

»It is only when the form is fully clear that your spirit will become clear.«
Robert Schumann

T

An alternative to a vertically arranged navigation bar is the horizontal bar.
A horizontal navigation bar leaves more space for information within the navigation area, but it has the disadvantage that it can impair the overall structure of the website if it is arranged in the centre.

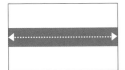

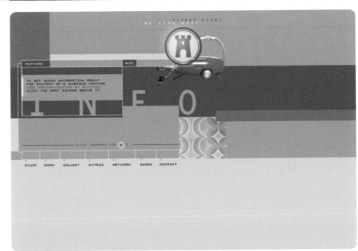

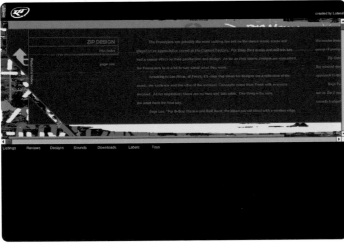

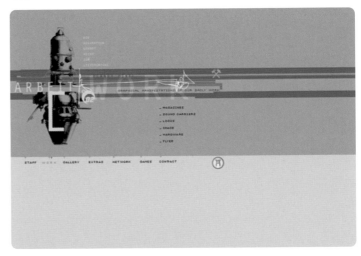

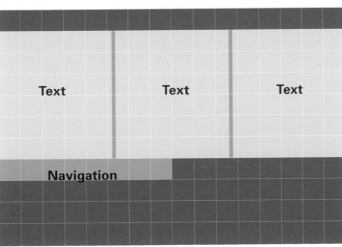

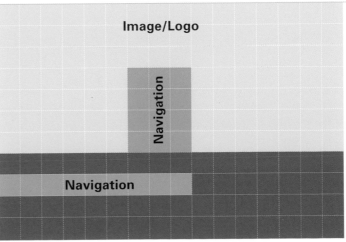

10.0

11.0

Navigation bar positioned vertically in the middle.
And full-screen navigation

A central vertical navigation bar, like a central horizontal bar, is suitable for pages with low information content and a lot of pictures, or only short texts.

The full-screen navigation is only suitable for individual pages. Repeated exposure to large selections of interactive options would end up confusing the user.

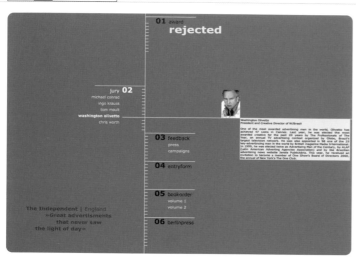

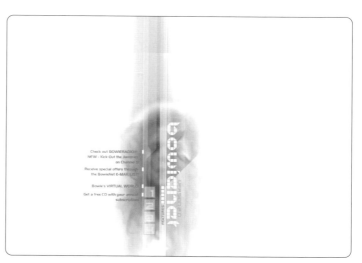

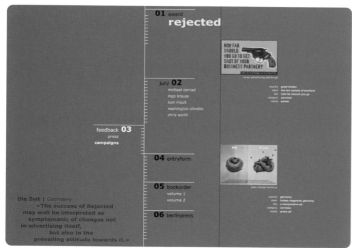

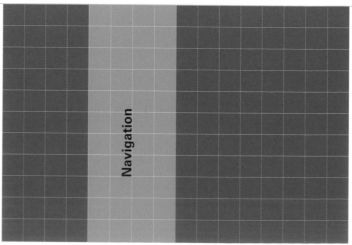

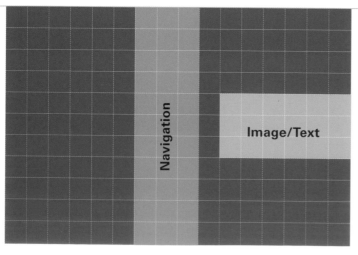

»A fish can concentrate for as long as nine seconds:
Mouth open, mouth closed, and eyes always wide open:
that is about all a fish can register.
And web-surfers?
Their span of concentration is declining steadily
– to the level of goldfish.«

Der Spiegel

A navigation bar which covers the full width of the screen is more suitable for start pages or pages which consist entirely of pictures.

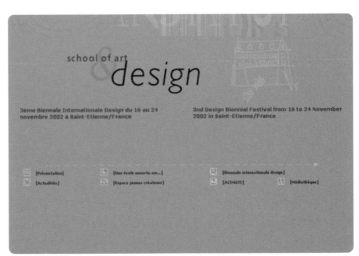

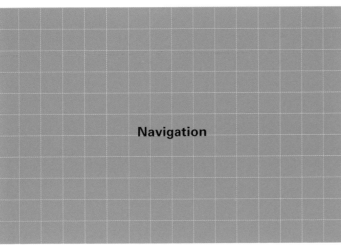

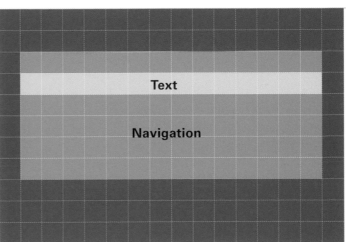

14.0

15.0

3.05

Grids for the screen
Distribution on a screen
Print and visual versions

For exclusive use on computers (visual version) a width of 595 pixels can be used for the display area. The maximum width of a printed version should not exceed 535 pixels.

Maximum pixel dimensions for print-outs (1.1) | in pixels

Width 535   **Height** 295   **pixels**

Distribution on a 640 x 480 pixel format

Before creating a website, the website designer must consider exactly who constitutes the target group of the information. The text length is then defined. The guiding principle here is less is more.

There are websites which are only designed to be viewed on the screen, others are designed to archive or print information.

If a web page contains a lot of text, it should always be designed so that users who want to archive the text or do not want to read it on screen can print it easily. If we use up the maximum pixel width which is suitable for display on screen, the reader who prints out texts will find that about two centimetres are missing on the right edge of the print-outs. The maximum pixel width for print-outs should not exceed 535 pixels.

By contrast, the maximum pixel width for display only on the screen can be as much as 595 pixels. These values already take into account the space needed by the browser.

Special attention should be given to the colour design: if the text and the background have a similar intrinsic brightness, this can lead to problems when printing with black-and-white printers or with printers set to print in black and white (2.1).

2.1 similar contrast   2.2 good contrast

Maximum pixel dimension for use exclusively on the computer (1.2) | in pixels

Width 595   **Height** 295   **pixels**

A typical example for a visual version:
Lots of graphics on a colourful background.

A typical example for a printed version:
Lots of text on a white background. On paper, longer texts are easier to read because of better resolution.

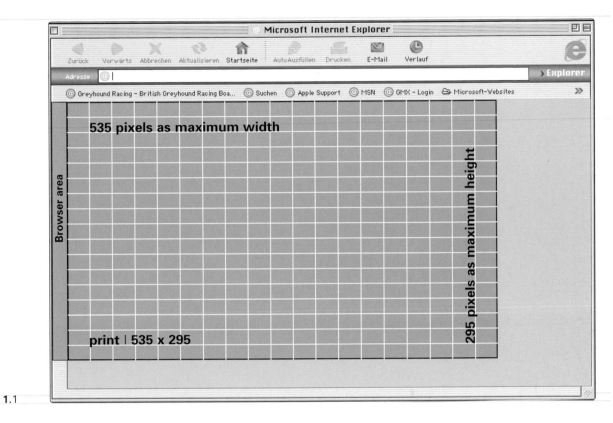

535 pixels as maximum width

Browser area

295 pixels as maximum height

print | 535 x 295

1.1

1.2

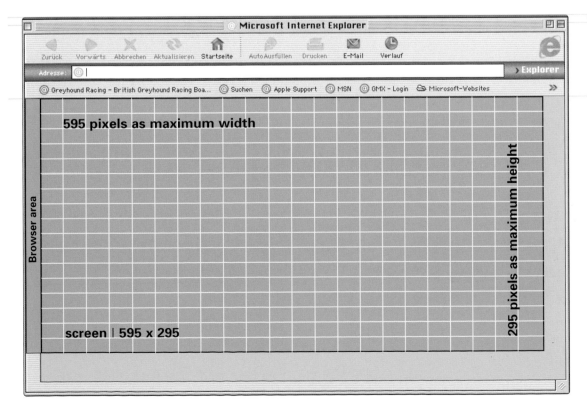

595 pixels as maximum width

Browser area

295 pixels as maximum height

screen | 595 x 295

3.06 Grids for the screen
Layout elements
Rollovers, Pull-down menus, Frames

Rollovers, pull-down menus and pop-up windows are typical interactive elements that can be used to make a web page more spacious and improve overall screen structure.

With this rollover the colour of the text of the menu items changes when the cursor moves over it.

If the cursor moves over the icons on the Saatchi website, the image in the square increases and thus provides feedback for the user.

Here the menu items light up.

Rollovers
Simple buttons can soon get boring. Rollovers are elements which fulfil the same function as buttons, but which are more interesting because they provide feedback and offer a wider range of design opportunities. They react for example by changing colour when the cursor moves over them.

Rollovers, pull-down menus and frames offer ways of organising digital presentations that are not available for (static) paper.

Pull-down menus
This way of arranging menu items saves a lot of space on the screen and offers a quicker overview of the main topics. Only the titles appear. If the user clicks on one of the menu items then a window opens temporarily with sub-menu items from which the user can then make a selection.

I am the Devil when I'm here;
I am God when I'm outside.

MIDALIA, 54

The website of the magazine »colors« uses the principle of the pull-down menus for images: the viewer's attention is attracted by the detail of the eyes. By clicking on the narrow section the entire portrait rolls open with a short statement.

| MYGOLF | HOTELS | CLUBS | PACKAGES | SERVICE | SHOP | KONTA |

Austria Map
Suchen

Vorarlberg
Tirol
Kärnten
Steiermark
Salzburg
Oberösterreich
Niederösterreich
Burgenland

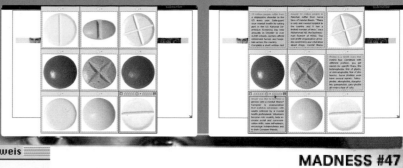

The windows of the »colors« website open as browserscript hints. They do not help to structure the contents, but act as a means of communication in order to increase the sensibility for the topic. Only when the reader has clicked on the »ok« button is it possible to move on.

Here, too, attention is drawn to the contents by using windows that open against an unchanging background.

Frames

Frames on a screen can be used to distinguish between basic information (which remains in the background) and current information (which appears in a window). These windows are usually smaller than the background and are vector-defined so that they are independent of the size of the monitor screen. Pop-ups are small windows that open up temporarily to provide topical hints and news when a web page is opened.

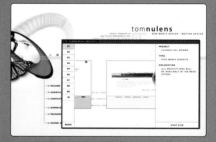

Items from the main menu in the background can be opened up in a separate window, which then pushes its way into the foreground without covering the main menu. The windows can be navigated independently. This arrangement adds considerable clarity to the website.

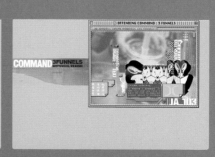

The website on the left offers two links on the home page that both open in their own window.
In this way two companies can be presented against the same background.

3.07 Grids for the screen
Innovative grid solutions
Linear Grids

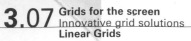

The linear grid includes a navigation bar as a standard element. The only thing there that changes is the selected information, and this is the interesting feature of a website.

Intro
The website of the photographer Rui Camilo, www.rui-camilo.de, presents itself in a systematic grid. The page is very simple in structure, aesthetic and functional, with special features in its details.

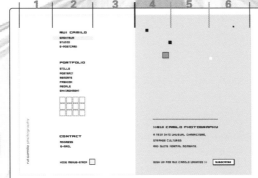

When the page is loaded, an area sub-divided into sixths appears. A sixth on the left of the screen contains the navigation. The right half of the page contains an area with a green background which shows changing information, text and pictures.

The special features of this website are found in the details.
For example, if the visitor selects the menu item »Studio« he can experience a virtual tour of the studio. He can make the picture move to the left or right, and magnify or reduce the scale of the picture cut-out.

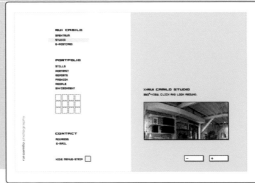

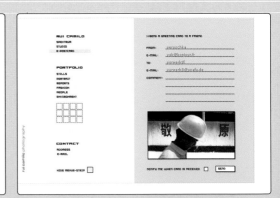

The menu item »Address« not only calls up a simple written address, it also shows a pictorial address. Small cars drive on the motorway near the studio – a simple animation with a great effect which is an attractive and unexpected detail and remains vivid in the memory.
To involve the visitor, there is a menu item which invites the user to send an »ePostcard«.

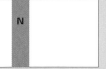
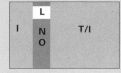

RUI CAMILO

SPEKTRUM
STUDIO
E-POSTCARD

PORTFOLIO

STILLS
PORTRAIT
REPORTS
FASHION
PEOPLE
ENVIRONMENT

DEERROOM

CONTACT

ADDRESS
E-MAIL

HIDE MENUE-STRIP

I : Image
L : Logo
N : Navigation
O : Orientation
T : Text

The design of the menu elements is very subdued and underlines the focus on the important items: the photographs themselves. The menu bar becomes transparent at the item »Portfolio« which shows the work of the photographer and is superimposed on the photograph that is displayed without completely covering it. The guidance in the navigation is clear and unambiguous: the menu item that is selected is highlighted in green. While the user is viewing the first photograph that has been loaded, the next photographs are loaded in the background.
In a box on the menu bar in which each photograph is symbolised by a small square, the current photograph displayed on the screen is marked in dark green. Photographs that are already loaded are marked light green, the square for the currently loading photograph blinks. Unloaded photographs are still white. Below the box, which provides helpful guidance, the user is given details of the photograph.

CAFE IN MACAU

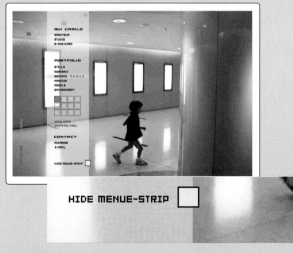

HIDE MENUE-STRIP

The website can be viewed as a full page without the menu bar if the user selects the option to hide the menu bar.
It then remains as a small button which follows the mouse and can therefore be moved to any position. When the button is clicked, the menu bar opens again.

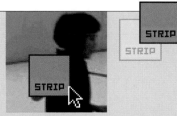

STRIP

STRIP

STRIP

3.07 Grids for the screen
Innovative grid solutions
Grid hierarchies

A grid at various levels: the basic structure remains the same, whereas the information in the left part (navigation) and right part (information) can be exchanged depending on the interaction. The levels are colour coded so that the user does not get lost.

Fonds BKVB

Subsidiemogelijkheden

Fonds in cijfers

Aanvraagformulieren

Begrippen

Links

Veel gestelde vragen

Agenda

Jaarindex

FONDS VOOR

BEELDENDE KUNSTEN

VORMGEVING

EN BOUWKUNST

BASISSUBSIDI

STIMULERINGS

BEMIDDELAAR

INTERREGELIN

INNOVATIE CO

BUITENLAND A

Intro
The split structure of this website shows that it is possible to present a lot of information without making things boring or confusing. This is done with a clear matrix and a colour guidance system: the basic layout of the website hardly changes except that the colours adapt to suit the content area and the information on the right is replaced. The navigation departs refreshingly from the common buttons such as »Contact«, »FAQs«, »Profile« etc.

Feedback:
If you click on the logo to return to the overview page, it changes colour.

1 Navigation   **2 Information**

The content presented is clearly structured:
The top left eighth of the page:
The logo, which is also the navigation back to the overview page;
the colour of the logo describes the **different areas.**
In the eighth next to the logo:
The area clicked on is enlarged as a heading, in the colour for the area.
In the quarter below the logo and the heading:
The sub-navigation for the heading
In the right half:
The information asked for, in text or picture form.

Colours are ideal to establish and arrange a matrix without intricate structures and to create links.

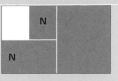

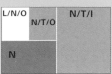

I : Image
L : Logo
N : Navigation
O : Orientation
T : Text

If there are large amounts of text, the remaining text which is not visible can be brought into view by scrolling.

The colours change depending on the information area. The layout of the rest of the page remains basically unchanged.

Fonds BKVB
Subsidiemogelijkheden
Fonds in cijfers
Aanvraagformulieren
Begrippen
Links
Veel gestelde vragen
Agenda
Vacatures

English summary

FONDS VOOR BEELDENDE KUNSTEN VORMGEVING EN BOUWKUNST

Nieuws

Leestafel

Tentoonstellingen en debatten

BASISSUBSIDIES
STIMULERINGSSUBSIDIES
BEMIDDELAARSSUBSIDIES
INTERREGELING

INNOVATIE COMMISSIE
BUITENLAND ATELIERS
STUDIEREIS BOUWKUNST

OEUVREPRIJZEN EN
BENNO PREMSELAPRIJS

When the user goes to the first overview page of the Dutch art subsidies website, www.fondsbkvb.nl, he or she is given three navigation bars.
When he or she clicks on a link, the logo increases in size to cover all of the top left quarter of the page. It is used for navigation to enable the user to return to the overview page after calling up information from the three navigation bars.

3.07 Grids for the screen
Innovative grid solutions
Grid hierarchies

Even if the grid structure is not clear to the users it is still possible to provide guidance and ensure that the users do not get lost. Grid elements in the wider sense of the term, such as colour or a specific way of presenting the pictures can also be used as design features.

Intro
The Dutch Society for Old and New Media, www.waag.nl, presents its website almost completely without grids, however the site does not appear disorderly. The horizontal navigation bar along the top is a repeated element, along with the transparency of the Waag building. The colour scheme, with orange, black and shades of grey, gives the presentations their characteristic appearance.

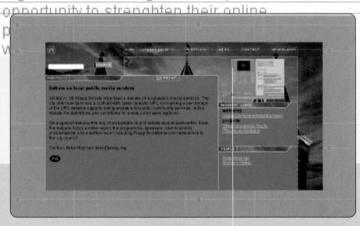

The website reacts individually depending on the subject area: where there is a large amount of text, it extends over the whole page. For smaller amounts of text, e.g. in the presentation of website examples, the text can be scrolled within an area. The main focus here is on the row of pictures passing across the screen. By clicking on a miniature, the user can see an enlarged picture and a detailed description on a new page. If that is not enough for the user, he can also go directly to the website.

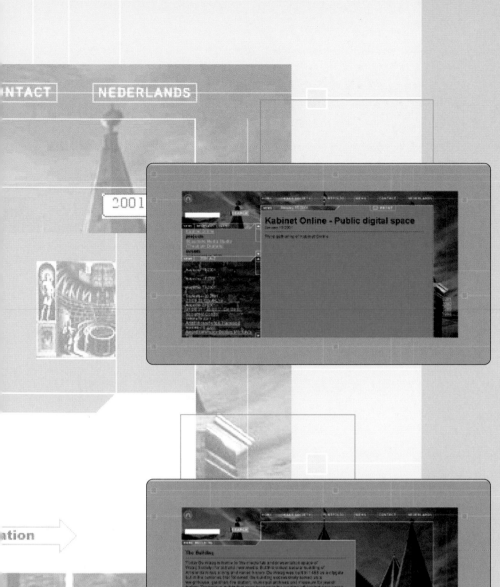

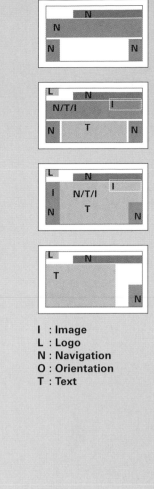

I : Image
L : Logo
N : Navigation
O : Orientation
T : Text

In spite of the different sub-divisions of the navigation bar and the information elements, the website does not appear fragmented. In these three examples, coherence is assured by the identical width of the text area. This is also supported by the colours: we perceive colours even before we notice the structure of the page, so they have an identification effect.

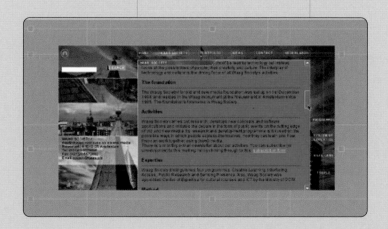

3.07 Grids for the screen
Innovative grid solutions
Grid hierarchies

A clear, fixed grid makes it possible to find items
such as the navigation bar even when they are
placed in an unusual position, for example on the
right edge of the screen. The changing information
on the left is then at the focus of the user's attention.

Intro
This website is built up around a rather unusual arrangement of the navigation bar, which is situated on the
right of the picture above the logo. Once the navigation
bar is loaded it remains unchanged, and an overview
of the area selected appears in the top left window. To
provide orientation for the user, a brief text showing the
subject area appears at the same time in the bottom left
panel. If the reader is interested in obtaining more information, he can click the desired object in the overview,
and it is then shown in detail in the middle left panel of
the matrix.

The reader is offered two information levels:
One level provides the general overview and
is shown in the top left part of the matrix.
After the user clicks on the desired object,
detailed information is shown enlarged in
the matrix window below the object.

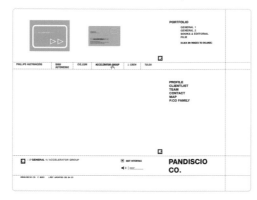

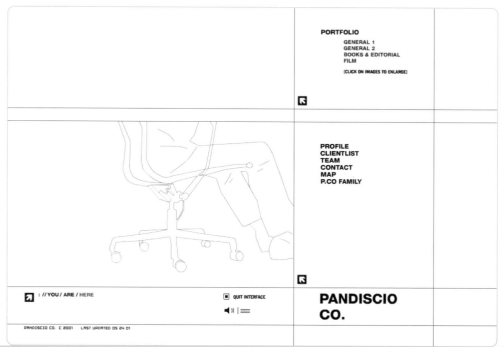

The website of the New York design company,
www.pandiscio.com, is striking for its clarity of structure and simplicity. The structured layout of the matrix
means that the website is clearly organised without
needing to include additional guidance elements such
as colours as an ordering feature.

Colour is used very sparingly:
only where it is essential for recognition (i.e.
here the colours of the subway stations), as
feedback for the navigation and of course for
working examples.

PORTFOLIO

GENERAL 1
GENERAL 2
BOOKS & EDITORIAL
FILM

[CLICK ON IMAGES TO ENLARGE]

»Ornaments make me sick.
How much beauty can emanate
from type and its distribution.«
Hugo von Hoffmannsthal

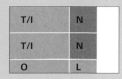

I : Image
L : Logo
N : Navigation
O : Orientation
T : Text

To show which link the user is currently under, there is a brief summary consisting of key words in the bottom left matrix window.

: // GENERAL 1 / ACCELERATOR GROUP

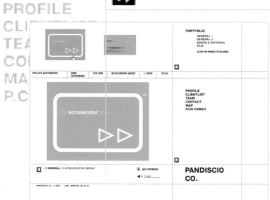

// BOOKS & EDITORIAL / VANESSA BEECROFT

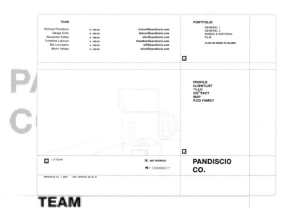

TEAM

chard Pandiscio   → [READ]
Takaya Goto   → [READ]
Alexander Kellas   → [READ]
mothee Letouze   → [READ]

Feedback:
If a function has been selected it is highlighted in colour (blue) and the text is displayed larger as feedback for the reader to show that the required step is being carried out.

anners,
orld of
t at

hed
s for
eers

If the text is long, the hidden text can be brought into view by scrolling within the window.

3.07 Grids for the screen
Innovative grid solutions
Grid hierarchies

Levels can be used to distinguish between navigation and information, but also to distinguish between different types of user: the professional user, or the less-experienced hobby visitor. The aesthetics are adapted to suit the level in question.

Intro

The website of mutabor design company, www.mutabor.de, is presented at two user levels: the experienced surfer can alter settings with a remote control and overview the entire site before making selections. The other level offers more assistance, and guides the less-experienced user in easy steps.

The guided user level: The user is encouraged to select one of the circles on the corners of the triangle. This circle then grows larger and shows the topic. The sub-menu items scroll slowly through the circle and can be read. A topic can then be clicked and loaded.

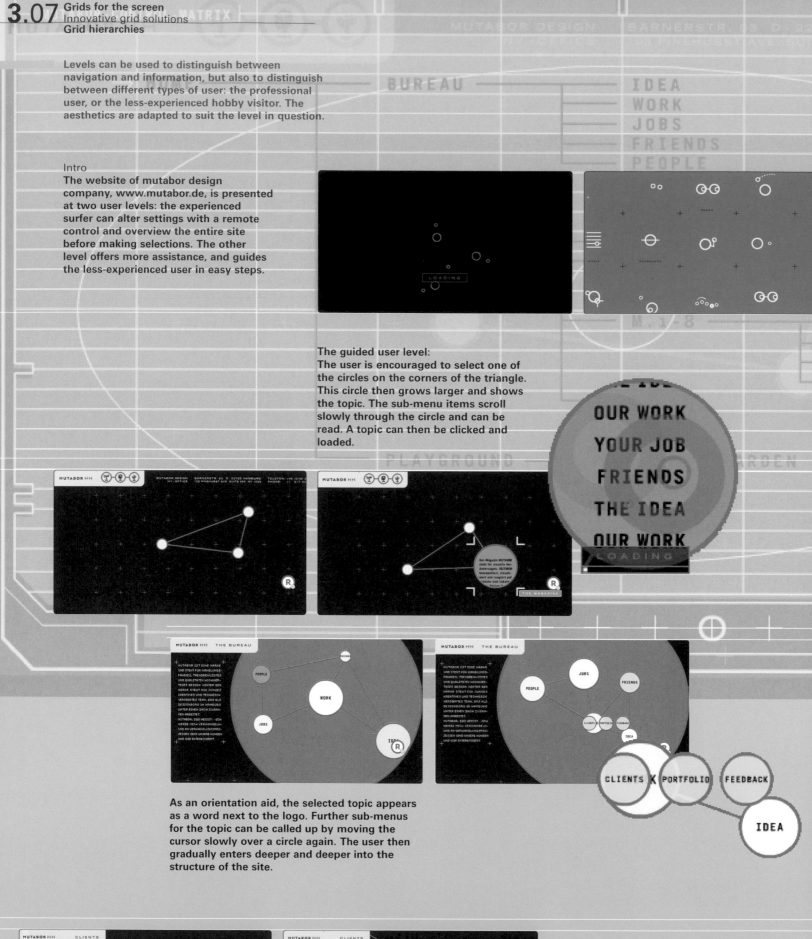

As an orientation aid, the selected topic appears as a word next to the logo. Further sub-menus for the topic can be called up by moving the cursor slowly over a circle again. The user then gradually enters deeper and deeper into the structure of the site.

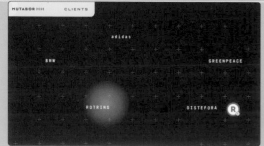

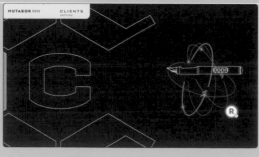

The pages with examples are the same for both user levels, but the user is guided there slowly in the one case, and quickly in the other case, by-passing intermediate steps.

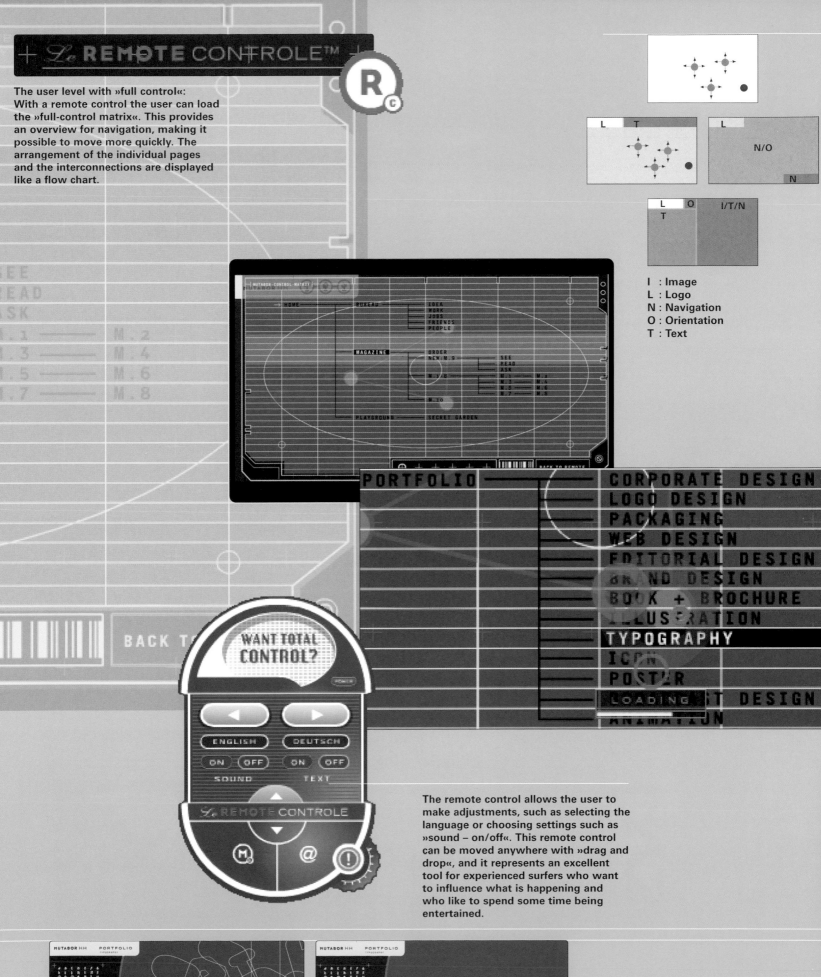

Le REMOTE CONTROLE™ Ⓡ

The user level with »full control«:
With a remote control the user can load
the »full-control matrix«. This provides
an overview for navigation, making it
possible to move more quickly. The
arrangement of the individual pages
and the interconnections are displayed
like a flow chart.

I : Image
L : Logo
N : Navigation
O : Orientation
T : Text

The remote control allows the user to
make adjustments, such as selecting the
language or choosing settings such as
»sound – on/off«. This remote control
can be moved anywhere with »drag and
drop«, and it represents an excellent
tool for experienced surfers who want
to influence what is happening and
who like to spend some time being
entertained.

3.07

Grids for the screen
Innovative grid solutions
Fluid grids

A flexible structure is not synonymous with lack of structure. The grid constants can be related to a system of colour codes and repeating elements, which always work according to the same pattern and thus establish a functional and aesthetic unity.

Time **travel**

72   48   30   20   bpm

Intro
The website of German design company www.nasa20.de has a flexible structure. The information that is offered appears in small windows, each of which is internally navigable and can be moved anywhere on the screen. The windows appear on a subject-oriented background which contains additional clickable options and quotations.

//UPDATES/ HOT STUFF

13/12/2001
IF DESIGN AWARDS WWW.NASA20.COM STRIKES A

19/11/2001
N.A.S.A.2.0 HAS BEEN SUCCESSFUL AGAIN

13/11/2001
LIAA 2001 - THREE FINALISTS - NO AWARDS

16/10/2001
N.A.S.A.2.0 SITE GET REWARDED

09/10/2
WWW.TW

04/10/2
N.A.S.A.2

24/09/2
EVERYBO

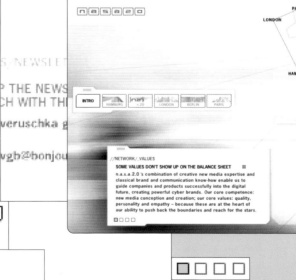

//REFERENCES/INTRO
THE WORLD OF WORK
At n.a.s.a.2.0 creativity and quality are what count most. Since the net knows no limits, neither does our thinking. Which is why there is only one idea for n.a.s.a.2.0: the best!

Only this one idea can assert itself at n.a.s.a.2.0.

The year was still 11 minu
The Julian year lasted 365

//NETWORK/. VALUES
SOME VALUES DON'T SHOW UP ON THE BALANCE SHEET
n.a.s.a.2.0's combination of creative new media expertise and classical brand and communication know-how enable us to guide companies and products successfully into the digital future, creating powerful cyber brands. Our core competence: new media conception and creation; our core values: quality, personality and empathy – because these are at the heart of our ability to push back the boundaries and reach for the stars.

I'LL BE ALWAYS WITH YOU.

The square opens the menu as a roll-over menu when it is clicked. It acts as a sort of wizard in that it follows the cursor to any position, makes comments and offers ways to change the content level by clicking.

UPDATES
NETWORK
REFERENCES
JOBS
FREESTYLE
CONTACT
X

Orientation:
Where there is a greater amount of text within a box, several small squares appear, and the number of squares gives an indication to the amount of text in the box. The user can click the next square to move to the next section of text. Colouring of the relevant square shows which text level the user is currently in.

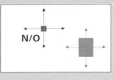

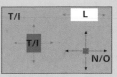

I : Image
L : Logo
N : Navigation
O : Orientation
T : Text

»Even chaos is grouped around a fixed point, otherwise it would not exist even as chaos.«
Arno Schmidt

Simplicity of operation:
Because of the wizard, the small square that constantly follows the cursor and the simple operation of the functions on the website, the user does not lose the general overview in spite of the high level of flexibility. The information is presented in the form of buttons, and when they are clicked they open a window with the required content. It is possible for several windows to be open at the same time, and this is indicated by the colour of the buttons (black). The open windows can be clicked away as required.

//UPDATES/_HOT STUFF

2001-12-13 | HAMBURG

IF DESIGN AWARDS: WWW.NASA20.COM STRIKES

For the sixth time this year (ADC Deutschland, ADC New York, British Design & Art Direction, New York Festivals, London International Advertising Awards) www.nasa20.com got rewarded at a renowned design award: the jury

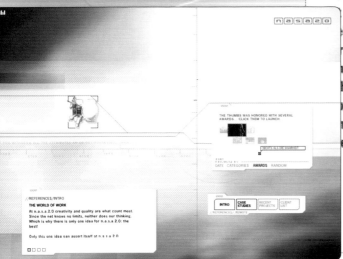

[← BACK CONTACT

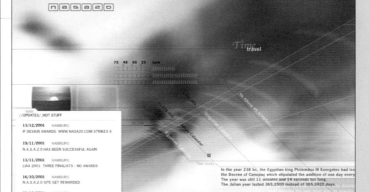

The windows can be moved anywhere on the screen by »drag and drop«. The reader can thus move about on the information level of Nasa 20 – here »updates« – or call up the next level which contains entertaining information about different time calculation systems.

3.07 Grids for the screen
Innovative grid solutions
Fluid grids

Even with a static basic structure, a website can
create the impression of a fluid (that is non-linear)
grid if every interaction leads to visual changes.
Changes are possible in every grid field, determined
from the various navigation fields.

Intro
The website of Twix »it´s all in the
mix«, www.twix.de, unfolds as a
separate, smaller window against the
Twix background. This means that the
navigation can be placed at the right
edge of the window and the text and
image area on the left. The animated
DJ skilfully guides the user to the
navigation area which is less
favourably positioned.

Special details:
In spite of the simple
structure, the user does
not lose interest in spending
time on the website. This is
achieved by the stimulating
animation of the navigation,
the DJ and the interesting
build-up of the information
area. When text and pictures
are loaded they appear offset
and moving, which maintains
the curiosity and motivation
of the user to see what will
come next.

UNTER MEINEM MISCHPULT FINDEST DU
DIE NAVIGATION.PROBIER ES AUS + GET
IT ALL IN CHECK!

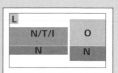

Every change made to the content also brings about visual change. In spite of the rather static structure of the website, it does not become boring. In the Twix history section the appearance of the DJ changes to match the period, the hairstyle of the period becomes a symbol and period-related pictures are enlarged. Without leaving the information panel,

the user can navigate through time by using a small white box on the time bar.

I : Image
L : Logo
N : Navigation
O : Orientation
T : Text

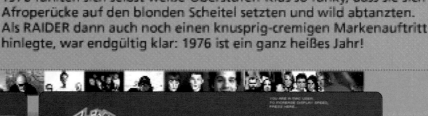

Afros, RAIDER und der Funk   1976

Das war ein aufregendes Jahr: Die Funk-Welle erreichte ihren absoluten Höhepunkt, und die Tanzböden kochten unter hippen Plateauschuhen. 1976 fühlten sich selbst weiße Oberstufen-Kids so funky, dass sie sich eine Afroperücke auf den blonden Scheitel setzten und wild abtanzten. Als RAIDER dann auch noch einen knusprig-cremigen Markenauftritt hinlegte, war endgültig klar: 1976 ist ein ganz heißes Jahr!

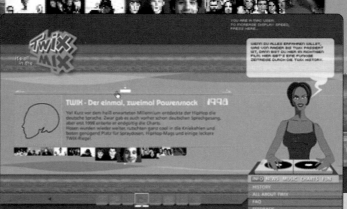

The navigation is divided up into three areas:
• The position below the DJ desk. It acts as a text menu and a »roll-over« menu, i.e. the sub-menu is only visible when the user goes to the permanent bar with the mouse.
• Navigation which moves horizontally through the picture: it consists of small pictures. The white bar can be pushed on from one picture to the next;

the corresponding information is then opened up. This pictorial navigation also has a guiding function.
• The navigation within the information area. It appears as a text menu, a button or a scrolling feature, as necessary.

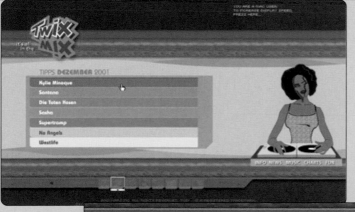

3.08 Grids for the screen
Dos and Don'ts
Dramaturgy

Screen pages create a clear impression when they
form part of a closed system that is
easy to understand. Functional and hierarchical
elements (not more than seven per page) can
support this impression. Sites can be interesting
if the elements can be played off against each other
and the sequence of individual pages maintains a
dramaturgy.

1.1
Despite the many elements on the website
of Deutsche Post, the overall effect is not
confusing. The use of background colours
leads the eye and gives structure to
the elements. This is supported by a
clear grid orientation of the elements.

Dos and Don'ts
Dramaturgy

A well thought-out site works in much
the same way as a play in the theatre:
the sequence of events is arranged so
that interest is maintained as they
unfold.

The storyboard

It is usually very helpful when producing
a site to draw up a flow chart diagram to
visualise the various possible sequences
of use, and the way interest and tension
develop through them – like the
storyboard for a film for example (see
pages 78–83).

Creating inner balance

The information and visual effects
offered by a site need to be well-
balanced – the site should not be
overloaded, but neither should it be
patchy and uneven. As a designer you
should take care to ensure that not
more than five to seven elements are
included on any one page. Any more
than this will mean that elements cannot
be clearly distinguished, and items will
be overlooked so that the information
cannot be registered and structured.
When a site is overloaded then the
user will be less willing to concentrate
on the contents, and will retain less
of the information. Another obvious
drawback is that a packed site offers
little space for subsequent expansion or
updating.

When the elements have been defined
they have to be arranged into a
hierarchical order so the user can
be guided along. For example, a
hierarchical arrangement might involve
the use of different sizes (large/small),
animations (moving/still), or a suitable
colour scheme.
Recurrent elements, such as a logo, can
be set in a grid so that the user will find
them quickly and always in the same
place. For important functional elements,
a good placement is in the top left-hand
corner of the page, since this is where
people usually look first, and it is never
affected by the size of the screen or the
browser that is being used. A consistent
use of a grid will ensure that the functional elements for navigation and orientation are always found in the same place,
and this will make the reader feel more
confident about the contents provided,
as well as making it easier to move
around. However, such a set-up may
seem too static for some purposes. If a
more dynamic or fluid effect is needed,
then the designer might turn to a grid
that does not involve fixed positions,
but that uses other signals such as
colour codes, or recurring animations.

»Hippocrates gives two examples which
enable us to understand all disharmony;
they are being too full and being too empty.«
Paracelsus

The start page of the mutabor site provokes
the viewer with pulsating elements, symbols
and concepts. Whatever associations are
clicked – »smell«, »taste«, »multimedia«,
etc. – open the main page. A variety
of elements can animate the user and
encourage a playful approach.

Websites with a clear design can get by
with fewer than seven elements.

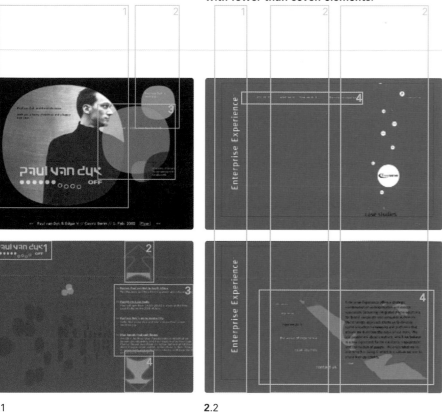

.1   2.2

Mutabor's »secret garden« page teaches the
user how to get about the site efficiently, so
that the following pages do not need as
many text elements and explanations.

Small icons which have already been
explained can free a site of superfluous
text and make it easier to understand.

3.08 Grids for the screen
Dos and Don'ts
The User

The first impression often decides which user groups will be attracted to a website. Surfers tend to prefer sites with striking graphics that offer entertainment and complicated animations, whereas irregular users of digital media tend to look for less spectacular sites, and attach more importance to the information contents.

FUNNILY ENOUGH: HUMANS ARE NOSY BY NATURE. YOU ARE NOT.

1.1

Dos and Don'ts
The user

Before designing a grid system it is important to think carefully about the targeted users and the contents that needs to be provided.

Future users: who is who?
People may use digital media for many different reasons. Users who want to be entertained react positively to a different type of website than those who are looking for information.

The web surfer is on the look-out for striking sites that can be animated and are colourful. The information contents is often only of secondary importance. These users generally regard web surfing as a leisure activity. In this case, lots of colour and animation can be used even though it will slow down the down-loading process. Flash pages are almost a »must«, as is a suitable musical sound-track as backing (2.1–2.3). The grid chosen on the basis of these considerations should be flexible, and able to support sound, colour, and animation, along with little surprises (1.1) – the user will have seen many sites and will easily get bored. The elements integrated in the grid, such as buttons, and the language of the menu items should be appropriately »cool«.

2.1

2.2

2.3

3.1

3.2

The occasional user, who sees digital media as a source of information, is looking for clear structures and ease of use. An uncluttered arrangement with a rigid grid system and rapid navigation to the required link are essentials (**3.1–3.2**). The peripheral attributes that digital media can offer, such as sound, animation and kaleidoscopic colour should only be used very sparingly. This may make things easier to master for the less experienced visitors to the site, but importantly it also shortens the download times, which **busy users** will appreciate. Well-designed HTML-pages are ideal for meeting these needs. The situation is similar for **experts** using digital media to search for information: they are not interested in entertainment, but want to find what they are looking for as quickly as possible.

In contrast to the occasional user, experts are familiar with such sites, so they can be offered a grid construction which allows them to skip superfluous menu items.

With **the international user** in mind, the terms used should be easy to understand (**4.1**). Care should be taken with the colours used, because their connotations can differ widely from culture to culture. Other items such as date formats must also be clearly defined (**4.2**).

By carefully considering the design goals in advance, selecting appropriate structural elements, and providing more or less information, it is therefore possible to target the website, and this will influence how long the user will use it, and whether or not they will return to it again later.

»Express your idea in a clear sentence.
If you are unable to do that,
people will suspect that you have no idea.«
Sean K. Fitzpatrick

philosophie **philosophie**
wie we zijn
projects **projekte**
projecten
contact **kontakt**
о нас
philosophy
проéкти
projects
контакт
contact

4.1

4.2 04·03·03 03·04·03 04·march 03

3.08 Grids for the screen
Dos and Don'ts
Colours | Navigation | Orientation

Colours presented on screen need to be handled carefully: their appearance can vary greatly on different systems. Too much colour can have a confusing effect and the contrast needs to be chosen so that there is no glare. Large graphics take a long time to download, it is better to use smaller images that do not keep the user waiting.

Digital media usually offer an open system, so the orientation needs to be unambiguous in order to ensure trouble-free navigation.

If a website has a patterned background the text has to have sufficient contrast. This can be achieved with contrasting colours, or as shown here by means of focus...

...or by a special window that opens for the information...

1.1

Dos and Don'ts
Colours, graphics, backgrounds

Too much colour and flashing elements tend to be counterproductive when it comes to attracting attention to a specific aspect of a site.
The availability of an endless array of colours – free from the cost constraints found in print publishing – naturally represents a considerable temptation. But this makes it all the more important when determining the use of colours to have the interests of the target group in mind, as well as the effects of the colours and colour combinations.
The choice of the colour of the text in relation to the background colour is very important, especially since text is more difficult to read on screen anyway.

The web designer must pay attention to good colour contrast and the text must not be blurred by a very bright background. If there is too much going on in the background this can distract from the information provided in the foreground.

Well-designed websites work:
It can be annoying when complicated graphics make the loading process very slow. It helps if information is given about how the download is proceeding and when it will be completed, or if some entertainment or information is provided to help pass the time.

T¹
White text on a dark background can easily disappear if the background has not been loaded.

T²
Colours are not necessarily the same across different platforms: On an Apple Mac a colour tends to appear brighter than the same colour value on a PC.

2.1

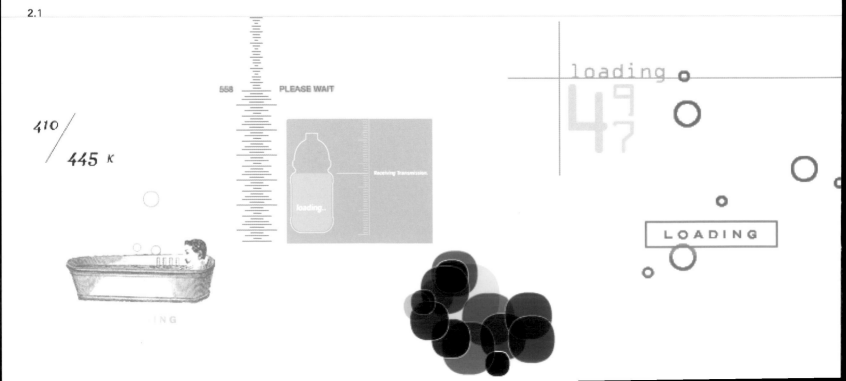

410 / 445 K

558 — PLEASE WAIT

Receiving Transmission.

loading..

loading

LOADING

I N G

T¹

It is wrong to assume that the website you can see on your screen will look the same everywhere else. Depending on the graphics card used, the window-size of the browser and the setting selected by the user, there can be considerable differences in page sizes, positions and colours.

The colours, fonts and font sizes are determined by the browser or the viewer: given all the variables, the production of a website is very different from determining the appearance of an end-product in print publishing.

...or due to very low contrast in the structured background against which the text stands out clearly.

Colours can help to structure a website if they are allocated appropriately.
On the left:
orange: new publications
On the right:
green: up-to-date subjects

3.1

T²

In order to establish a grid it is best to begin with the position of the navigation unit and a page that includes the most text or images. The design of the remaining pages will then follow on from this.

T³

Using modular units, the designer can create a flexible, but recognisable structure.

Dos and Don'ts
Orientation and Navigation

It is by no means guaranteed that users will arrive at the front page of a website. A search machine may direct them almost anywhere. It is therefore important that each page can be understood in its own right, and that there is always a clear link to the starting page.

Every page should have a navigation element, this helps with the orientation and gives the user the certainty of being able to move backwards and forwards and jump about without getting lost. Feedback and orientation aids, including graphics, icons or short summaries also form important elements of a good navigation structure.

An attractive website should offer logical and predictable connections, though it can include surprises when it comes to the detail.

As a rule, the navigation should not be positioned far to the right or in the lower part of the frame. Where this is unavoidable, then attention should be drawn to it, for example by an animation, special colours, or striking icons, etc.

The clearly structured website of clever.co.uk is able to turn the rules on their head: a grid gives all the elements a strictly arranged layout, only the navigation elements are capricious. But by assigning white as a colour code, they stand out against the red background and black text and can easily be identified as the navigation.

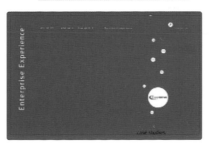

3.08 **Grids for the screen**
Dos and Don'ts
Scrolling | Text on the screen

Limited scrolling can help to keep things clear, and will make it easier to navigate. As an alternative to scrolling, information can be provided on a number of pages. But it is important not to separate notes from the text they are referring to.

Digital media are regarded as modern, dynamic means of communication. Users expect that the texts should also be fresh and lively, and that the labels used, for example for links, should be short and easy to understand.

»Birds in migration find their way south precisely because they do not reflect on how they will get there.«
Werner Heisenberg

Dos and Don'ts
Scrolling – or less is more

Very few users are patient enough to scroll all the way down a long text, so the scroll function should be used as little as possible.
Avoid combined vertical and horizontal scrolling completely, because it is too demanding. If scrolling has to be used, then it should only be in one direction, and at the end there must be a button to jump back to the start, so that it is not necessary to scroll all the way back again. During scrolling, the navigation elements should not disappear. The scrolled text should not exceed 763 x 444 pixels. An alternative is to split a longer text up into pages and to provide a well-designed orientation bar under each page.

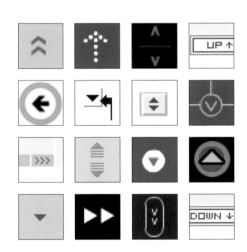

Scroll arrows should be clearly distinguishable from program scroll bars in order to avoid any confusion. With an appropriate design, it is still possible to integrate them in the overall layout.

Examples of symbols that can be used as orientation aids for the paging function.

Examples of symbols for the »jump-to-top« function.

Dos and Don'ts
Menus and links

An aesthetically pleasing grid can still lead to disappointments if the details have not been thought through in advance.

Overused items in menus such as »About us«, »Contact« or »FAQs« may be recognised quickly and easily, but they can easily seem commonplace and unexciting. The same holds for a command like »click here«. It pays to consider carefully exactly the target group for a website, and what the site has to offer. Is it possible to think of more interesting alternatives for menus and commands which are just as clear and unambiguous?

When it comes to including links in text, the rule once again is: less is more. There is a great risk of distracting from the text itself with excessive underlining and colours. One alternative is the use of well-designed icons. These have the advantage in some circumstances that they are easy to recognise.

Internet users are impatient: they want to get to information quickly and to know where they are. Teasers, which should contain no more than three sentences, can be used to attract the reader to a topic. The follow-up text should be short, clear and well-structured.

FRESH FROM THE FARM

the slophouse   the harvest   farmhands   the homestead   farming methods

Icons from advertising agency »concept farm«
www.conceptfarm.com

Icons from Internet agency »bloomingdales«
www.bloomingdales.com

Icons from Internet agency »lollibomb«
www.lollibomb.com

raw materials   manufacturing   product

Icons from advertising agency »tbwa«
www.tbwa.com

3.09 Grids for the screen
Front pages
Analogies of printed covers

In most cases the start-up page will be the first thing that a user sees of a website. It can be purely visual, containing only essential information, much like the cover of a book, or it can be more like the cover of a magazine, with information about key items of content.

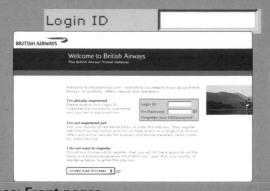

A good front page already defines the grid structure for the pages that follow, such as the array of elements, colour schemes, etc.

A special case: Front pages

The starting page has the function of providing the user with an introduction and an overview, as well as allowing preliminary navigation, for example with the selection of the preferred language. It extends a welcome and says: This is where something new starts. A good front page can generate interest, with the message that the following contents will be useful and relevant, so that users are encouraged to look further. Sometimes this crucial first impression is completely spoilt by long downloading times, poor graphics, uncreative graphic elements (another set of waving flags for the choice of language) or poor structure, so that the users are not interested in clicking on any of the offers.

Some people argue that a starting page is a waste of space, because it often contains little more than the logo and a welcoming message. But by using an interesting structure, contents and graphics, designers can make sure that there is no vacuum.

**The better known a company is, the less information is needed on the starting page. In such cases it might even be dispensed with altogether.
The less well-known an enterprise is, the more information is needed on the starting page – as a minimum its aims and objectives.**

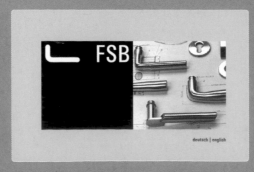

Pages with a primarily functional character, for example pages of a search engine or service pages of airlines, do not need a starting page: the emphasis here is on speed to access information.

Key information: book cover

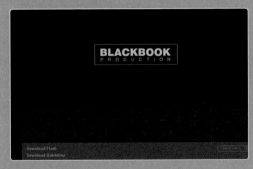

Overview: magazine cover

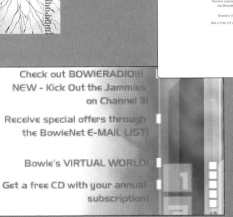

Start pages can be designed as decorative introductions providing just the key information – like a book title. Or they can be like the cover of a glossy magazine with what is essentially an overview of the contents.

3.09 Grids for the screen
Front pages
Start pages in grids

From the existing grid for the website it is possible to derive the start page.

The attraction of starting pages should not consist solely of large graphics, because these can take too long to download, and some users will be dissatisfied before they have even started.
It is possible to create a good impression with the use of background colour, text and small graphic elements, but with very acceptable downloading times.

The website of Eskedahl Design is a good example of a grid that is well thought out. The start page defines the constants which are then enriched with information on the following pages. The grid remains the same. On the start page the user already gets to know the navigation bar and the parameters for guidance through the site. By contrast with the following pages, the start page has very little information, carries the logo and is thus recognisable as the start page.

Integration of the starting pages in a grid
The starting page should only be designed after the grid and all the elements for the following pages have been determined. The front page will usually be formed on the basis of the structure of the information pages.

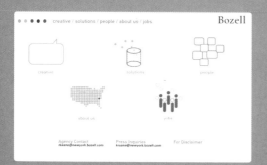

The Bozell start page is not governed by the same grid as the following pages, but it uses a systematic colour and icon structure. The icons and the associated colours of the various menu areas are introduced on the **start page and then used on the following pages to help the navigation.**

»An interface not only has something to do with the look and feel of a computer.
It is just as concerned with the creation of a personality,
the design of intelligence [...], capable of perceiving
human sensibilities.«

Nicholas Negroponte

Young & Rubicam's start page has a blue background and white text. On the following pages the colour is only used marginally: the colour scheme is reversed. The information text is blue on a white background, but the navigation remains on a blue background.

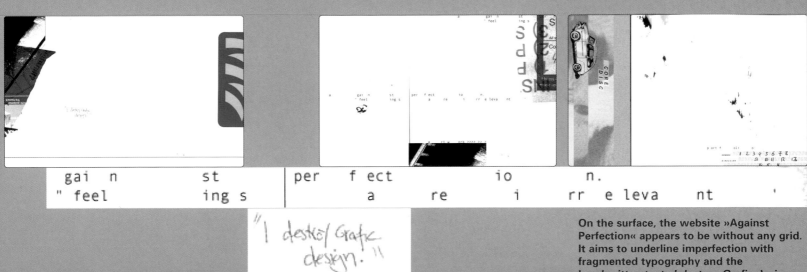

gai n   st
" feel   ing s

per   f ect   io   n.
            a   re   i   rr e leva   nt

" I destroy Grafic
design. "

On the surface, the website »Against Perfection« appears to be without any grid. It aims to underline imperfection with fragmented typography and the handwritten text »I destroy Grafic design«. But here too there is a grid, although it is a vague one. That of grace – determined by the minimalist approach, the repetition of the colours, and the destructive element. This is a constant theme through all the pages.

3.10 Grids for the screen
Banners
Integration in a grid

If additional items are brash and flashing, then they can distract from the main information provided by the page. But interesting elements outside the frame can attract and bind the attention of visitors to the site.

Positions of advertisements with a high CTR (Click-Through-Rates).

Advertisement next to the menu bar.

Advertisement next to the vertical scroll bar.

Advertisement in the second third of a page.

If possible banners should not be placed on the first page. Banners can significantly increase the loading time because the first page usually also includes other graphic elements. This could annoy the user and even make them cancel the loading process.

Flashing banners may have a high attention value, but in time they become annoying and leave the user with an uncomfortable feeling.

Banners

Banners are usually rectangular areas on web pages which contain static or animated information or advertising, and in the latter case they have a link to the advertiser. The position of a banner must be chosen carefully because the reader may be irritated reading the content if the banners constantly flash or twitch. The click to the advertiser can also be achieved more intelligently, for example if the reader can actively edit the banner and thus become involved in the content of the advertising – without any need for obtrusive animation.
But it is better to leave out the advertising completely, because it takes up space and is not the reason why a person visits a website.

Banner formats	in pixels
Full banner	468 x 60
Half banner	234 x 60
One third banner	156 x 60
OMS banner	400 x 50
Vertical banner	120 x 240
Micro button	88 x 31
Button	120 x 90
Button	120 x 60
Large button	130 x 80
Small button	137 x 60
Small square	75 x 75
Square button	125 x 125
Skyscraper	120 x 600
Wide skyscraper	160 x 600
Rectangle	180 x 150
Medium rectangle	300 x 250
Large rectangle	336 x 280
Vertical rectangle	240 x 400

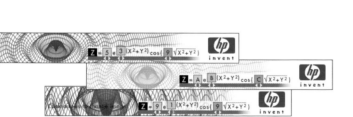

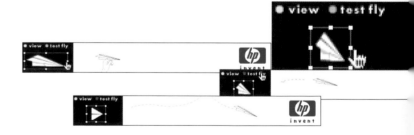

Interactive banners
An example of good banner design:
The banners used by HP have a flowing and calm animation. The user can actively change the banner by adjusting the values in the mathematical formula, which in turn changes the colours and figures.

Interactive banners
Another example of good banner design:
Here, again, the banner is not a twitching distraction. It calls on the viewer to be interactive and build a paper plane, and then to carry out a virtual test flight.

When a page is opened, the pop-ups often appear briefly in the top left corner where they are noticed better. But the position in which they then settle is the bottom right corner.

Pop-ups of different sizes.

Alternatives to the banner

ausblenden ×

Banners, which are often only clumsily integrated into an overall grid, can also be designed differently. Alternatives to the banner can include an extra window, a so-called »pop-up«, on the start page. This is a smaller browser window without the usual buttons and icons. Pop-up windows are often designed to open automatically when a page is called up. They contain advertising or topical information and can be turned off at will.

A text display is another alternative. The text display is similar to editorial advertisements in magazines and is usually at the end of the text on a website. If the advertisements are informative, they will also be accepted by the viewer. They are not only acknowledged more than banners, they are also clicked more often.

49

49

A globe floating over the website is an alternative to banners.

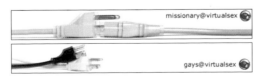

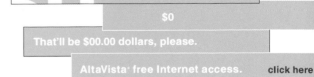

Interactive banners
The plain and cheap appearance of the banner design is used by a car dealer to give the impression that the viewer can find a bargain when buying a car.
On the banner the viewer can choose a brand of car and the year, and this skilfully guides him to the car dealer's website.

Innovative banners
Using otherwise familiar pictures in a novel way can create impact. When combined with simple animation, the viewer's curiosity can be aroused.

Aesthetic banners
Most banners are conspicuous in their poor design. Too many colours, too much animation and too many font types are almost characteristic of banner design. This example shows that banners do not have to be like that. Banners can manage very well without a large number of colours and excessive animation.

The design of a CD-ROM is very similar to that of a website. Here once again special rules apply for the screen, in contrast to those for print publications. But the CD-ROM has the advantage that it is not dependent on a browser: there is more reliability on the appearance of the final product than there is for a website.

Intro

The contents of this CD-ROM on the Persian language adheres closely to a systematic grid. This makes the presentation clear and easy for the users of the CD-ROM. The well-planned grid makes it easier for the screen designer to arrange and structure the contents. Visual logic must not be boring, because the visual sensation can lie in the detail, as can be seen in this example.

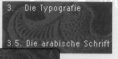

Despite the unfamiliar impression created by the use of Persian numbers and the structure of the main menu from right to left in accordance with Arabic script, the reader does not become disoriented. If the cursor is moved over a Persian number then a small text box opens with an overview of the point by way of orientation. This is always at a standard position on the left side. The user can enjoy the fascination of exploring the unknown without becoming disoriented.

The area of 832 x 624 pixels of the CD-ROM »Die Persische Schrift« is backed by a grid with 9 x 8 units. Within this area there is a smaller section of 550 x 400 pixels, with 6 x 5 units. This creates two main axes, a horizontal and a vertical, which are suitable for arranging text, images and animation and allocating functions.

Almost every technology that is suitable for setting up a web page on the Internet can also be used to produce a CD-ROM. As on the Internet, it is possible to integrate images, sound, video, text and interaction on a CD-ROM. Of course it is not possible to link up directly to other websites, but on the other hand it is not necessary to worry about browsers, Internet connections, etc. The most common program used is Macromedia Director. It can be started directly from the CD-ROM in order to present the contents.

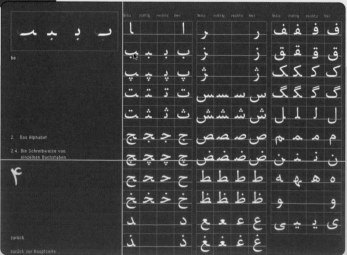

The image doesn't always have to be static – animations are also possible. The captions are not altered for each animation, but the current number is highlighted from a list of all animated logos. This helps the viewer to keep track of the logos that have already been seen, and the ones that remain to be looked at.

Music and sound can be used as grid elements, for example in order to give the user feedback or to attract attention. When animations appear these are backed up with Persian music.

The text is always to the left of the vertical axis or beneath the horizontal, but its exact position can be varied according to the image and the length of the text.

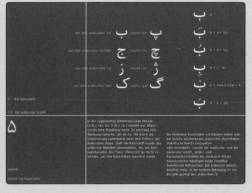

The size of the images and the layout as well as the column width of the texts are determined by the grid.

4. The numbers
4.2. Overview

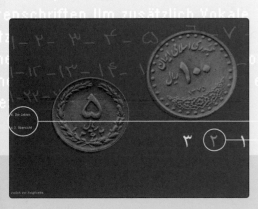

The efficient hierarchy from main menu to sub-menus and its menu items helps with visual identification so that the user is soon able to move around confidently.

The text is extended to a column width of three units.

3.11 Grids for the screen
CD-ROMS
Grid cells and colours

CD-ROMs are often used for instructional purposes.
A clear, minimalist grid helps to make the contents
easier to understand: the designer just needs a few
well-chosen grid cells and a colour coding system.

spatial reorientation
room orientation +
room reorientation +
floor reorientation ++
assignment to a line +

spatial recovery
fragmentation +
recovery
temporal order ++

compression

isometric

pattern

Intro

The CD-ROM »Innovation Techniques« by
William Forsythe has a clear interface and is
easy to use. Direct access is provided to all
the available topics. The user can
navigate using the buttons integrated on
the screen or has the option to pull down a
menu from the horizontal bar at the top
of the screen.

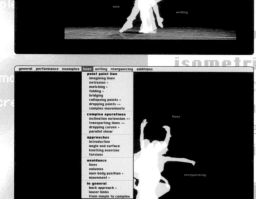

The CD-ROM is divided into a theoretical
part (marked with a »t«) and a performance part (marked »e« for examples).
The symbols »t« and »e« are present on
every screen, and a colour code shows
which part the user is currently in.
The performance example is marked
by a white »e«. If there are theoretical
explanations to that part of the performance then the »t« changes from black
to grey and can be selected, and the
theoretical explanations appear. Both
parts have the same grid with the same
main elements, which change colour to
aid orientation.

The time code bar makes it possible to obtain an overview of the
progress of the performance at any time. The user can see a
sequence again by pushing the pointer on the time code bar to
that sequence.

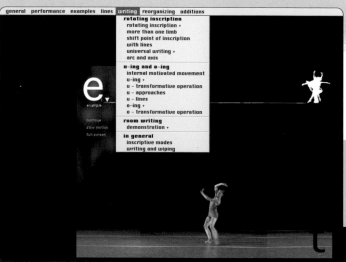

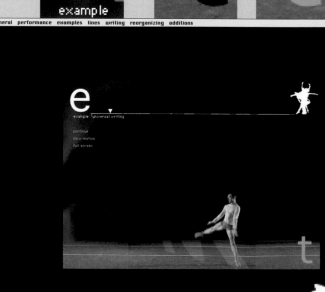

Symmetrical distribution:
The orientation and navigation are on the left and right, and the central section is where the action is.

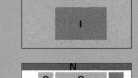

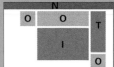

I : Image
N : Navigation
O : Orientation
T : Text

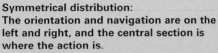

The principle of marking active and passive elements with colour codes is also used in the theoretical part: the displayed topics here are white and the passive ones remain grey. Using only these very simple elements it is possible to generate a very ordered appearance, and everything is easy to understand.

lines **writing** **reorgani**

point point line
imagining lines
extrusion +
matching +
folding +
bridging
collapsing points +
dropping points ++
complex movements

complex operations
inclination extension
transporting lines ++
dropping curves +
parallel shear

approaches
introduction
angle and surface
knotting exercise
torsions

avoidance
lines
volumes
own body position +
movement +

in general
back approach +
lower limbs
from simple to complex

solo

lines

point point line

complex operations

approaches

avoidance

in general

lines

volumes

own body position

movement

Certain topics from the theoretical section are linked to sequences from the performance and vice versa. When the user is in the theoretical part, the symbol for it is white. In this case the symbol for the performance part changes from black to grey when there are relevant examples.
The grid and its elements remain unchanged when switching back and forwards between the theoretical section and the performance examples.

In order not to destroy the uncluttered structure, and to keep things clear and concentrated just on the essentials, only an overview of the current contents is shown. The text always appears in the same place and is about the same length. The general overview of all the topics can be seen in a menu pulled down from the horizontal bar at the top of the screen, like in a computer program.
An alternative would be to use a scroll function, but this would introduce another dynamic element, distracting attention from the movement in the performance.

3.12 Grids for the screen
Mini-screens
Mobile telephones and hand-held appliances

Mini-screens do not offer much space for a clear grid structure, particularly if colour is not available as a code for functions.
The designer can make use of »traditional« symbols for the functions, and although these might not seem sharp because of the poor resolution, they will be readily identified.
Another option is to develop abstract symbols which look good, but then these will have to be learnt by the users.

Intro
On mini-screens, for example mobile telephones or personal communicators, the designer does not have much room, and the graphical means available are also limited – for example, colour coding is usually not an option – but there is still a large range of information to be presented. Generally speaking, the smaller the display then the tighter the logic and structure of the grid have to be, and the more important good icons and clear abbreviations become.

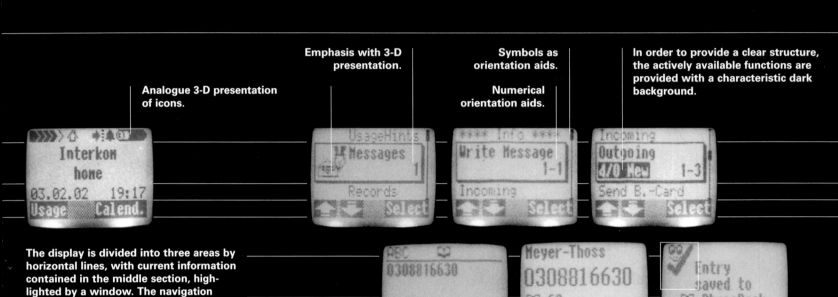

Analogue 3-D presentation of icons.

Emphasis with 3-D presentation.

Symbols as orientation aids.

Numerical orientation aids.

In order to provide a clear structure, the actively available functions are provided with a characteristic dark background.

The display is divided into three areas by horizontal lines, with current information contained in the middle section, highlighted by a window. The navigation elements are contained in the lower part, and the upper part is usually reserved for headers.

The three-dimensional analogue presentation of icons is quickly registered by the user, but it has the disadvantage that the icons can seem blurred if the display is of poor quality. Some widely-used symbols, such as a fountain pen, may create an old-fashioned impression in some cases.

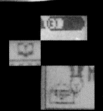

An organiser has a wide range of functions – many more than a typical mobile phone. This makes it necessary to organise information in a variety of different ways, such as the pull-down menu used here.

Most displays on organisers are still not in colour. Active functions are presented on a dark background in order to add emphasis.

The start-up setting is provided with simply-designed buttons in order to allow rapid orientation.

The symbols in the lower part remain unchanged. This allows the user to find and access frequently-used functions such as the calculator very quickly, or to jump back to the front screen. This section is intended to generate a feeling of familiarity and security for the user.

With mobile phones, the general idea is the smaller the better. But this places serious constraints on the size of the display, which is the interactive user interface. Most mobile phone displays now only measure about 35 x 25 mm.

Only the main menu items are provided with symbols. The larger font size makes it possible to highlight an item on the main menu.

Thanks to the clear organisation and the reduction of the information displayed, it is not necessary to provide icons for the items on the sub-menus.

Symbols as orientation aids.

Numerical orientation aids.

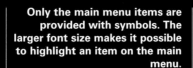

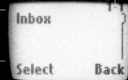

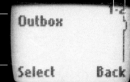

This display is also divided into three functional areas. The use of abstract icons and the reduction of the information content shown on the display at any one time help to create a tidy, modern impression.

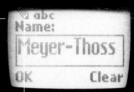

In order to distinguish it from the menu the name directory uses a small icon.

Hand-helds are used for organisation and they should work quickly and without hitches. This requires a display that is unambiguous and uncluttered (what sort of impression would a poorly-organised organiser make?).

This organiser display is divided into four parts: the upper part is used to indicate the function that is currently active, the section below this then shows this active function and the third contains the command bar. The bottom part, which remains unchanged, shows the frequently used organisational functions and the operational functions such as the zoom, or the display contrast.

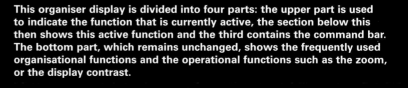

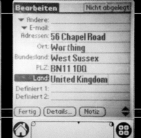

4.0 transfer of grids

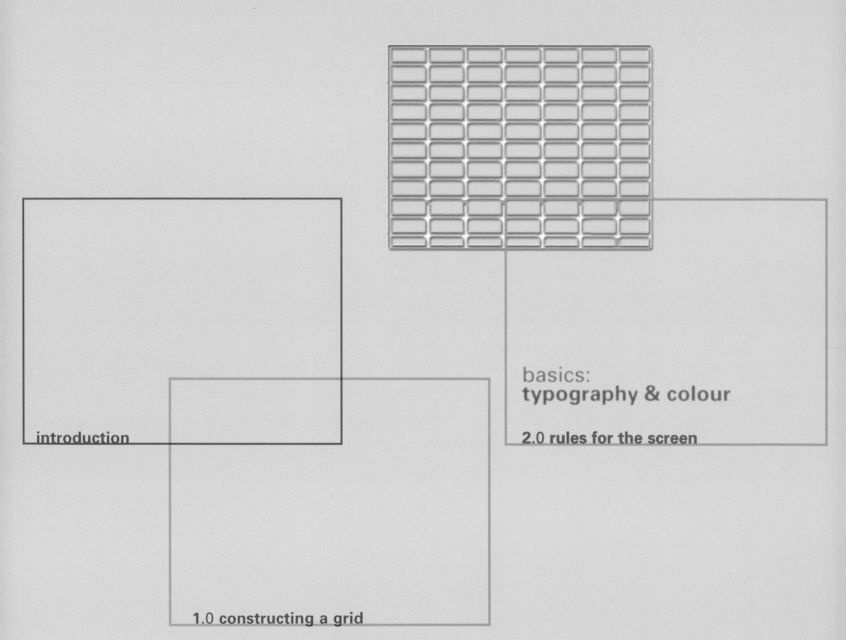

basics:
typography & colour

2.0 rules for the screen

introduction

1.0 constructing a grid

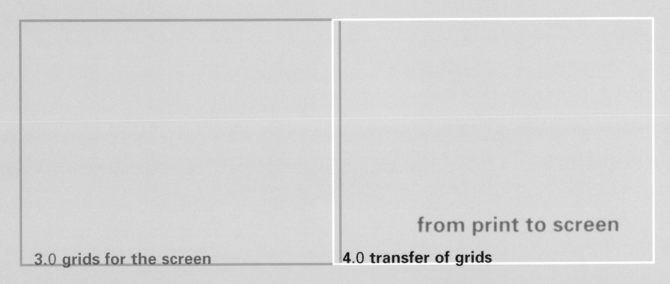

3.0 grids for the screen

from print to screen

4.0 **transfer of grids**

4.01 comparison: print, cd-rom, internet | 136
4.02 examples: print, cd-rom, internet | 138

4.01 Transfer of grids
Print, CD-ROM, Internet
Differences | elements in common

Transferring a grid from print to the Internet involves the same difficulties as the transfer from print to CD-ROM, i.e. that the grid cannot be transferred exactly. That is because of the technical properties and display characteristics of the different media. For example, the formats are usually different (portrait and landscape formats), and the resolution of the screen is inferior to that of print media. As a result, this affects the grid structure and therefore the typography. A grid can therefore only be »translated« in the wider sense, i.e. by the recognition factor for stylistic grid elements which are used in such a way that they fit into the respective medium.
In this chapter, the term »quotations« is used to describe excerpts taken from one context and transferred to a new context; in this case from print to new media.

Transfer of grid »quotations«

Picture:
»Quotation« of the picture and picture format.

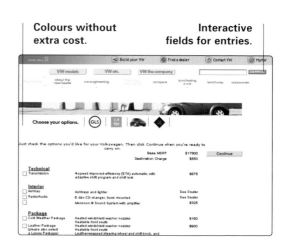

Even though the typographical grid and the text volume of a print publication cannot always be transferred exactly to a digital medium, the designer can nevertheless maintain the aesthetic impression. This can be done by using colours or by sparing »quotations« of typographic elements, even typefaces that are not ideal for the screen, if they are smoothed and used in large type sizes. The designer must decide in each case which stylistic elements are suitable for this »translation«.

Transfer of grids

In most cases a print publication exists first, and this publication is then transferred to digital media – the opposite is rare. By comparison with digital media, paper permits the free treatment of text and typography, e.g. the use of small type sizes and serif typefaces. But because of the poor resolution of the screen, small type sizes and serif typefaces are not so suitable for use in digital media. This in turn can affect the transfer of grids and defined CI (corporate identity) structures to the screen. Another issue is the format: print publications are usually in a portrait format and digital media in landscape format, and colours are not a cost factor for digital media as they are for print. And the possibilities of the two media are very different, because film, sound and animations can

only be integrated into digital media. These attributes mean that digital media tend to focus on images more than paper-based media, which tend to concentrate more on the content and text. But the perceptions of users and their expectations of the media are also different: users expect websites to be permanently revised and updated; in comparison with paper and CD-ROM, web presentations are the fastest medium that appeals to a general public. A website is entertaining and offers fast information, whereas more time is devoted to a CD-ROM, partly for reasons of cost, and the content is therefore often in greater depth than on a website. By contrast with websites, paper is used for archiving and thus has a longer »life«. Because of the different technical characteristics and their aesthetic effects,

---

Distinctive characteristics of print media | Catalogue

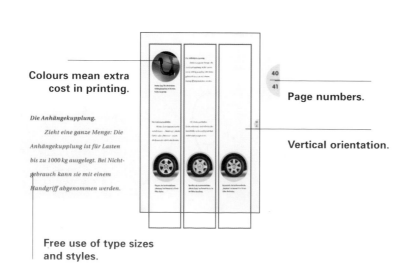

Colours mean extra cost in printing.

Die Anhängekupplung.

Zieht eine ganze Menge: Die Anhängekupplung ist für Lasten bis zu 1000 kg ausgelegt. Bei Nichtgebrauch kann sie mit einem Handgriff abgenommen werden.

Free use of type sizes and styles.

40
41
Page numbers.

Vertical orientation.

Distinctive characteristics of digital media | Website

Colours without extra cost.

Interactive fields for entries.

Type:

Type:
Use of the VW typeface
to maintain the CI.

**Large type sizes, use of
grotesque typefaces for
better legibility on
screen.**

Nice work.

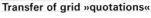

Aesthetic impression:
The lightness that is expressed by italic
type in the catalogue is expressed by light
colours on the website, because italic type
is difficult to read on screen. The grotesque
typeface used is displayed in grey to
transmit the lighter general impression.

Colour:
Use of the CI colour in the navigation bar.

Text | picture:
Text has been replaced by pictures (icons).
On the CD-ROM, text has been replaced by
spoken language. Here, on the website,
that would cause long loading times.

Transfer of grid »quotations«

a grid can therefore only be »translated
in the wider sense«, i.e. by the recognition factor for stylistic grid elements
which are used in such a way that they
adapt to the respective medium.

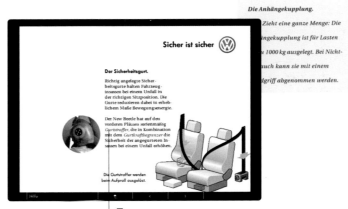

Type:
»Quotation« of an italic
type style.

Distinctive characteristics of digital media | CD-ROM

**Animation:
Film and sound.**

**Interactive list of con-
tents in picture format.**

**Pull-down
menu.**

**Narrow
text column.**

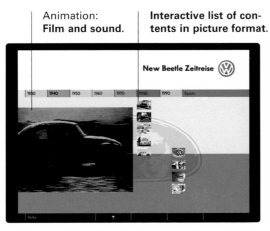

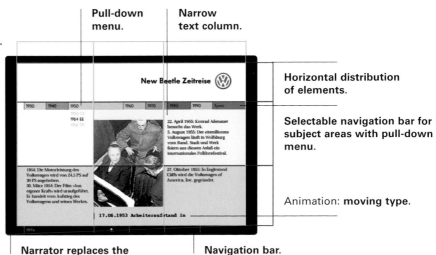

**Horizontal distribution
of elements.**

**Selectable navigation bar for
subject areas with pull-down
menu.**

Animation: moving type.

**Narrator replaces the
reading text.**

Navigation bar.

A grid cannot be transferred exactly from one medium to another. If the designer chooses »quotations« of the typical colours, pictures or typography of one medium and transfers them to the other medium, this maintains the aesthetic impression and thus the recognition value.

Intro

The transfer of a grid can be said to be successful if it has been adapted to the distinctive characteristics and possibilities of the respective media without losing the identity of an existing visual appearance. The design company »Porsche Design« is a good example of this.

The colouring, typeface and photographs on the website are the same as those used in the catalogue.

Catalogue: philosophy

The page in the catalogue which describes the philosophy of Porsche Design has the same information content in terms of text and pictures as the website. The linear sequence of the information in the catalogue (page after page) does not require navigation elements like those on the website, the space can be used simply for the two information elements, text and picture.

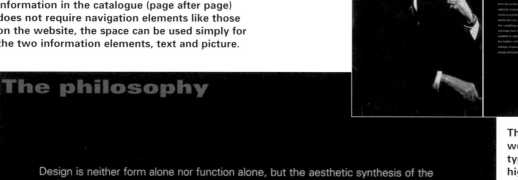

The catalogue has finer typography than the website: The typeface, type style, leading and type size can be freely selected because of the high resolution and the respectability of a print publication.

Website: philosophy

Porsche Design transferred the colours, text and pictures, but the typeface had to be adapted to the medium of the screen and extra functional elements were added on the website which were not needed in the catalogue: the functions of navigation and orientation in an open system.

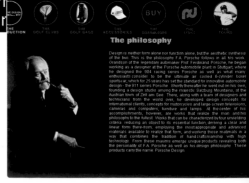

The colours, with white text on a black background, were taken over on to the website. They are suitable for good legibility in both media.

On the website, however, the type is not as fine as in the catalogue in relation to the resolution. The result is greater type size, smaller leading (to make space for the text volume) and a less sophisticated selection of typefaces and styles.

A website must contain more elements than a print publication. These extra elements are there to guide the user through a non-linear system and enable him or her to influence the display sequence interactively from any page. There are also functions which are not possible on paper, e.g. the possibility to enquire after current information or the provision of feedback to the user through changes in colour.

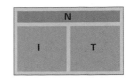

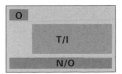

I : Image
N : Navigation
O : Orientation
T : Text

The possibility of obtaining current information.   Language selection.   Feedback by colour.

Catalogue: eyewear

The website is based on an overview of subjects on each page, whereas the catalogue shows the details on the page which need to be called up on the website. This principle of different depths of information on the website has the advantage that the scrolling and navigation by the user is kept to a minimum.

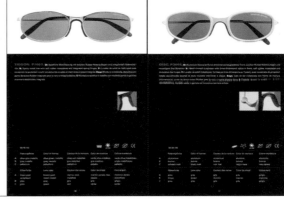

Website: eyewear

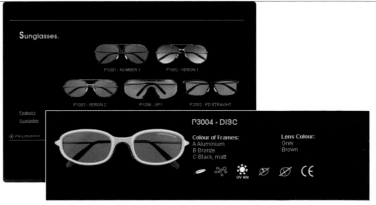

The introduction page of the website on the subject of »eyewear« is more complex in its information content than the cover of the catalogue. This is to enable the information to be grasped at a glance so that the user does not lose his or her bearings through excessive scrolling.

From the overview, items can be selected which are then magnified in a separate window and displayed with detailed information. This option, which enables the user to select the depth of information he wants to use, gives the presentation of the items greater clarity of structure.

Predetermined grid structures and CI characteristics of a print publication cannot be transferred one-to-one when designing a CD-ROM. And in addition, the CD-ROM offers the possibility of integrating sound and animations – which is something print publication cannot do.

Intro
The media presentation of Volkswagen's New Beetle has a very varied design. Information can be obtained from catalogues, CD-ROMs or on the Internet. The challenge for the designer is to achieve a sense of unity between the various products while taking into account the specific requirements for the various media and also the opportunities they offer.

The printed catalogue

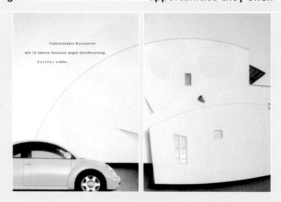

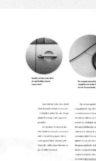

In the printed catalogue text can be read more easily in comparison with digital media. The texts in the catalogue can therefore be longer and provide a lot more information.

Der Regensensor und der automatisch abblendende Innenspiegel.

Ein Sensor an der Windschutzscheibe reagiert auf die Niederschlagsstärke und schaltet – nach

Das Technikpaket.

Wenn Sie Ihren New Beetle noch sicherer und komfortabler möchten, ist das Technikpaket genau das Richtige für Sie.

The use of an italic style and increased leading convey a light and carefree atmosphere, which matches the feeling experienced when driving a New Beetle.

Platz für sechs CDs: Der CD-Wechsler im Gepäckraum lässt sich über die Radioanlage bedienen.

28
29

Pagination is used as an orientation aid.

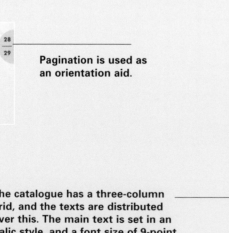

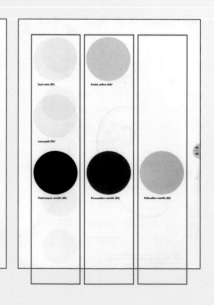

The catalogue has a three-column grid, and the texts are distributed over this. The main text is set in an italic style, and a font size of 9-point is used, which for printed matter is large enough to ensure that the product is easy to read. Very generous use is made of leading between lines.

In order to distinguish the captions from the main text, they are set in a different font, using a style with more colour and a slightly smaller font size (in this case 8-point).

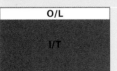

The CD-ROM

Hilfe	Lautstärke	Feedback	Beenden

Orientation on a CD-ROM does not require pagination;
instead a navigation and orientation bar is used.

O/L

I/T

Text displayed on digital media is often difficult
to read. Therefore less detailed content is provided in comparison with the printed catalogue:
the CD-ROM operates more effectively by
means of pictures and sound, and explains
concepts through animations.
A feeling of lightness was achieved for the
printed catalogue by the choice of font, but this
cannot be transferred directly to other media. A
similar effect is achieved on the CD-ROM by the
use of light backgrounds (white and light grey).

The vertical orientation of the column grid and
the line spacing used in the catalogue cannot
be transferred to the landscape format of the
CD-ROM, because it would involve excessive
use of scrolling, and the aim must be to present
the information so that it can be seen at first
glance. So the text has to be kept short,
and must be set without extra leading
between lines.

Ihr New Beetle ist in allen Sicherheits-
fragen auf Herz und Nieren überprüft
worden.
Lassen Sie sich von unserer Dummy-
...ver-
...eben.

Die maximale Schutzwirkung der
angelegten Sicherheitsgurte und
des Airbag-Systems wird nur in

Das Airbag-System.

Die *Front-* und *Seitenairbags*
bieten in Ergänzung zu den angelegten *Sicherheitsgurten* einen

| 10 | 20 | 30 characters/column |

The use of an italic style, which is not so easy to
read on screen, is restricted to key words, which
are coded in blue to show the user that further
information can be obtained at the click of a mouse.

Once again, a sans serif font is used for the picture
captions, but with less colour in the font style, because
small, bold text is not easy to read on screen. Similarly,
the headings are not in italic style. They are presented
in a bold sans serif font.

Airbags

The Internet aims at a more general and international audience than a CD-ROM. A website therefore needs a particularly easy-to-understand grid, navigation and guidance structure.

The CD-ROM

Intro
Compared with the catalogue, the CD-ROM and the website focus more on pictures. The website is more entertaining and appeals to a more general pubic than the CD-ROM, which is published as an interactive operating manual which concentrates only on the New Beetle.

The three navigation elements on the CD-ROM

Navigation bar to select the subjects.

Theme-based navigation bar.

Permanent navigation with general functions such as »Help«. It is situated below the information window itself. This is possible because the information window opens in a smaller format.

The information is distributed in such a way that scrolling is unnecessary and the page gives a clearly structured impression. Information is not only conveyed by pictures and text, there is also a voiceover. On the website, this would cause long loading times.

The CD-ROM and website are in landscape format, and thus horizontal. By comparison, the grid of the catalogue is vertical in structure, corresponding to a portrait format.

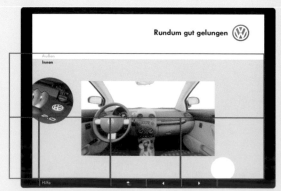

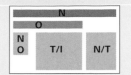

I : Image
N : Navigation
O : Orientation
T : Text

The grids for the website and CD-ROM are only similar in their horizontal orientation, although the screen is the medium in both cases. The reason for this is the different technical properties and concepts involved. For example, the website does not feature a voice-over mainly because of the more international target group, but also because the page would be too slow to load.

The website has a great breadth of information and is very up to date, whereas the CD-ROM concentrates on only one product and offers information which will be valid over a longer period.

The unifying factor is the »quotation« of grid structures and elements – the aesthetic impression. VW maintains the freshness of the visual impression by selecting white, blue and green as the colours of the items and using grey type.

The website

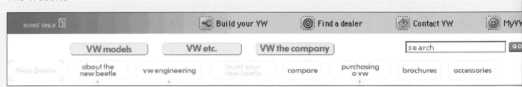

Elements which are not needed in the catalogue are very important on the website and CD-ROM: guidance to show the user where he or she is and navigation to show how to get from one page to the next. On the website, which aims to provide an overview of the whole range of products and services, the navigation is more varied than on the CD-ROM, which is limited to just one product.

The text on the website is split up into smaller chunks to make it easier to read and grasp. The website only uses the grotesque typefaces which provide better legibility on screen.

Wasn't that fun? And now you get to the best part – getting a quote. It's easy. Just save your car to your myvw page and send it off to the dealer of your choice. Don't have a

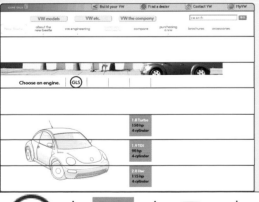

The website of the New Beetle offers flexible and interactive opportunities for the user which paper is unable to provide: the user can build his or her own car to his or her own taste, and then view it. To enable international users to understand the content better, many functions are displayed in pictorial form as icons, and not as text.

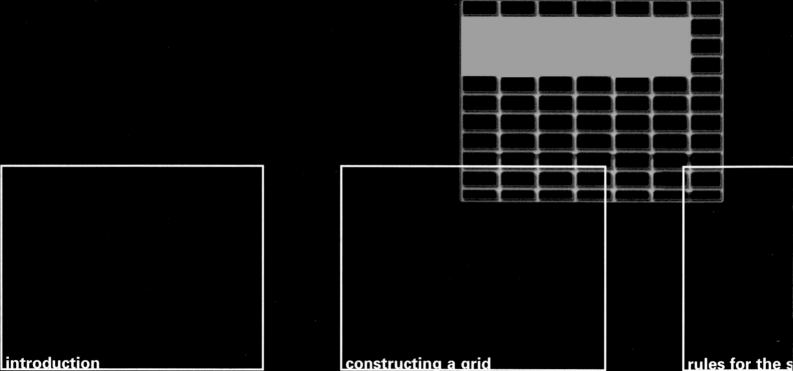

introduction

constructing a grid

rules for the s

grids for the screen

transfer of grids

Cyrus Dominik Khazaelis
Crashkurs Typo und Layout. Vom Zeilenfall zum Screendesign
Macintosh Werkstatt
Rowohlt, Reinbek, 1995

Joseph Müller-Brockmann
Rastersysteme für die visuelle Gestaltung
Niggli Verlag, 1996

Lewis Blackwell
20th century type | remix
Laurence King Publishing, 1998

Erik Spieckermann
**Studentenfutter oder: Was ich schon immer über Typographie
wissen wollte, mich aber nie zu fregen traute**
Context GmbH, Nürnberg 1989

Veruschka Götz
Color & Type for the Screen
RotoVision, Hove, 1997

Joe Gillespie
Webpage Design for Designers
www.wpdfd.com

Patrick J. Lynch, Sarah Horton
Web Style Guide
Yale University Press, 1999

Lynda Weinman, Jon Warren Lentz
Webdesign der Profis. Webdesign entschlüsselt in Fallstudien
Markt und Technik, 1998

Dieter K. Fröbisch, Holger Lindner, Thomas Steffen
MultiMediaDesign
Laterna Magica, München 1997

Daniel Donelly
www.design: web pages from around the world
Rockport Publishers, 1997

Petra Vogt
Erfolgreiche Präsenz im Internet. So machen Sie alles richtig
Smart Books, Kilchberg, 1998

Liesbeth den Boer
Geert J. Strengholt
Website Graphics: The Best of Global Site Design
Mediamatic, Amsterdam, 1997

chapter 1

019
Eugène Delacroix, 1798–1863, Painter
»Dem Auge ein Fest«, p. 107
(Diary, 6. May 1852)
Henschelverlag Kunst und Gesellschaft, Berlin 1979

021
Rainald Goetz, 1954– , Author
»Jahrzehnt der schönen Frauen«
Interview »Der Hauptkick kam durchs Internet«, p. 155
Merve Verlag, Berlin 2001

022
Stanley Morison, 1889–1967, Typographer
»Grundregeln der Buchtypographie«
Bern 1966

023
László Moholy-Nagy, 1895–1946, Painter and Photographer
hier zitiert in »Macintosh Werkstatt | Typo und Layout«,
Cyrus Dominik Khazaeli, p. 42
Rowohlt Taschenbuch Verlag GmbH, June 1995

024
Jan Tschichold, 1902–1974, Typographer
»Meisterbuch der Schrift«,
Ravensburg 1952

026
Ludwig Wittgenstein, 1889–1951, Philosopher
»Philosophische Untersuchungen«,
Werkausgabe Bd 1, p. 294
Suhrkamp 1995

030
Wassily Kandinsky, 1866–1944, Painter
in: Harenberg Lexikon der Sprichwörter und Zitate
Harenberg, Dortmund 1997

032
Tor Norretranders, Author
»Spüre die Welt. Die Wissenschaft des Bewußtseins«,
p. 99
Rowohlt, Hamburg 1994

034
Eugène Delacroix, 1798–1863, Painter
»Dem Auge ein Fest«, p. 86
(Diary, 10. August 1850)
Henschelverlag Kunst und Gesellschaft, Berlin 1979

036
Herbert von Karajan, 1908–1989, Conductor
in: Harenberg Lexikon der Sprichwörter und Zitate
Harenberg, Dortmund, 1997

Peter Jenny, 1942– , Professor of Design
»QUER/AUG/EIN. Kreativität als Prozess. Eine Schulung
anschaulichen Denkens«, p. 22
VdFV, Zürich 1989

041
Pjotr Perevesenzev
in: Harenberg Lexikon der Sprichwörter und Zitate
Harenberg, Dortmund 1997

chapter 2

044
Vincent van Gogh, 1853–1890, Painter
in: »Vincent van Gogh. Lebensbilder. Lebenszeichen.«, p. 18?
(Brief an Theo v. G., 4. May 1885)
Henschelverlag Kunst und Gesellschaft, Berlin 1989

045
Ad Reinhardt, 1913–1967, Painter
in: Harenberg Lexikon der Sprichwörter und Zitate
Harenberg, Dortmund 1997

047
Walter Gropius, 1883–1969, Architect
in: Harenberg Lexikon der Sprichwörter und Zitate
Harenberg, Dortmund 1997

048
Reginald von Durham, from the 12th century
in: »Kulturgeschichte der Farben. Von der Antike bis zur
Gegenwart«, p. 63,
John Gage
Ravensburger 1994

049
Dietrich von Bern, from a German saga
in: »Kulturgeschichte der Farben. Von der Antike bis zur
Gegenwart«,
John Gage
Ravensburger 1994

051
Eugène Delacroix, 1798–1863, Painter
»Dem Auge ein Fest«, p. 107
(Diary, 6. June 1851)
Henschelverlag Kunst und Gesellschaft, Berlin 1979

052
Nicholas Negroponte, Author
»Total digital«, p. 133
C. Bertelsmann Verlag GmbH, München 1995

063
Rainald Goetz, 1954– , Author
»Jahrzehnt der schönen Frauen«
Interview »Der Hauptkick kam durchs Internet«, p. 149
Merve Verlag, Berlin 2001

chapter 3

087
Albert Einstein, 1879–1955, Physician
    in: Harenberg Lexikon der Sprichwörter und Zitate
    Harenberg, Dortmund 1997

091
Robert Schumann, 1810–1856, Composer
    (Musikalische Haus- und Lebensregeln)
    in: Harenberg: Lexikon der Sprichwörter und Zitate
    Harenberg, Dortmund 1997

093
www.spiegel-online.de, On-line magazine
    Hamburg, March 2002

105
Hugo von Hoffmannsthal, 1874–1936, Author
    in: F. A. Kittler:
    »Aufschreibesysteme. 1800–1900«, p. 316
    München 1995

109
Eugène Delacroix, 1798–1863, Painter
    »Dem Auge ein Fest«, p. 107
    (Diary, 12. May 1853)
    Henschelverlag Kunst und Gesellschaft, Berlin 1979

111
Arno Schmidt, 1914–1979, Author
    in: Harenberg: Lexikon der Sprichwörter und Zitate
    Harenberg, Dortmund 1997

115
Paracelsus, 1493–1541, Alchemist
    »Ein Lesebuch nach seinen Schriften«, p. 279
    Will-Erich Peuckert (Hg), Leipzig 1941

117
Sean K. Fitzpatrick, Executive Vice President McCann Ericsson
    »Unpublished Best Rejected Advertising« Volume 1,
    Veruschka Götz (Hg), p. 68
    Grey Press Berlin, 1997

120
Werner Heisenberg, 1901–1976, Physician
    »Ordnung der Wirklichkeit«, p. 133
    Piper, München 1989

121
Albert Einstein, 1879–1955, Physician
    in: »Briefe an Maurice Solovine«, p. 128
    Berlin 1960

123
Stanley Kekwick, 1952– , Managing Director
    »Artbooks International«, London
    Frankfurt Book Fair 1999

125
Nicholas Negroponte, Author
    »Total digital«, p. 114
    C. Bertelsmann Verlag GmbH, München 1995

chapter 4

141
Rup Gussmann, 1958– , Musician and Performer (Philo Hip Hop)
    Berlin 2002

Index
Digital Media
Internet addresses
CD-ROM
Others

A

Aeroflot Russian Airlines, Russia
www.aeroflot.com
p. 076, 077
www.aeroflot.org
p. 074

Aidio Multimedia Assassins, USA
www.aidio.com
p. 118

Against Perfection, United Kingdom
www.against-perfection.co.uk
p. 125

AncientArtz, China/USA
www.ancientartz.com
p. 097, 122

Apple Computer, Inc., USA
www.apple.de
p. 054

Artistica, USA
www.artistica.org
p. 122

Atom Shockwave Corp., USA
atomfilms.shockwave.com/bin/content/
shockwave.jsp?id=stain06
p. 116

atomictv, United Kingdom
www.atomictv.com
p. 067

Audi AG, Germany
www.audi.com
p. 065

B

Bates Germany Werbeagentur GmbH, Germany
www.bates.de
p. 074

Sibylle Berg, Switzerland
www.sibylleberg.ch
p. 052

Berlin Press Verlags GmbH & Co KG, Germany
www.bestrejectedadvertising.com
p. 085, 092

Blackbook Production, Denmark
www.blackbook.dk
p. 123

David Bowie, United Kingdom
www.davidbowie.com
p. 092, 123

Boxfresh, United Kingdom
www.boxfresh.co.uk
p. 068

The Bozell Group, USA
www.bozell.com
p. 124

British Airways, United Kingdom
www.british-airways.com
p. 122

The Fifth International Browserday, Germany/Netherlands
www.browserday.nl
p. 108, 109

Buddha Graphix, Denmark
buddha.graphix.dk
p. 057

C

Rui Camilo Photography, Germany
www.rui-camilo.de
p. 098, 099

Francois Chalet, Switzerland
www.francoischalet.ch
p. 116

Clever Media, United Kingdom
www.clever.co.uk
p. 115, 119

Colors Magazine, Italy
www.colorsmagazine.com
p. 096, 097

The Concept Farm, USA
www.conceptfarm.com
p. 121

D

DaimlerChrysler AG, Germany
www.daimlerchrysler.com
p. 051

Yan Dehner, Germany
www.yantec.de
p. 088

Deutsche Lufthansa AG, Germany
www.lufthansa.com
p. 117, 122

Deutsche Post AG, Germany
www.post.de
p. 114

DFilm Digital Film Festival, USA
www.dfilm.com
p. 087

DHKY, Japan
www.dhky.com
p. 090

DJ Paul van Dyk, Germany
www.paulvandyk.de
p. 115, 118

DJ Rok, Germany
www.dj-rok.com
p. 086

DJ Tanith, Germany
www.tanith.org
p. 052, 053, 089

E

eboy, Germany/USA
www.eboy.com
p. 116

Ecole des Beaux-Arts de Saint-Etienne, France
www.institutdesign.fr
p. 093

Ecole de Communication Visuelle, France
www.ecv.tm.fr
p. 057

Editions 00h00.com, France
www.00h00.com
p. 119

Ekidna, Italy
www.ekidna.it
p. 116

Emirates, United Arab Emirates
www.emirates.com
p. 122

Erco Leuchten GmbH, Germany
www.erco.com
p. 026, 086

ESAG Penninghen, France
www.esag.tm.fr
p. 038

Monica Eskedahl Grafisk Design, Sweden
www.eskedahl.se
p. 041, 124

Euro RSCG Worldwide, USA
www.eurorscg.com
p. 064

F

Faber Castell (A.W. Faber Castell Vertrieb GmbH), Germany
www.faber-castell.com
p. 054

Frederic della Faille, Belgium
www.disparate.net
p. 055
www.disparate.net/invalid
p. 056

Floydsfollies – Animated Cartoons by Chris Bartlett, USA
www.floydsfollies.com
p. 045

Fonds BKVB, Netherlands
www.fondsbkvb.nl
p. 100, 101

Fountain/Peter Bruhu, Sweden
www.fountain.nu
p. 116

Franz Schneider Brakel GmbH & Co, Germany
www.fsb.de
p. 064, 122

G

Ganodesign, Italy
www.ganodesign.it
p. 076

Golf in Austria, Austria
www.golfinfo.at
p. 096

Google, USA
www.google.fr
p. 123

Graf D'sign, Russia
www.gdscb.com
p. 123

Graphic Obsession, France
www.graphicobsession.com
p. 056

Graphisme, Italy
www.graphisme.it
p. 123

HJKL

The Head Space Project, United Kingdom
www.head-space.com
p. 077

Hochschule für Gestaltung Schwäbisch Gmünd, Germany
www.hfg-gmuend.de
p. 038

Jaguar, United Kingdom
www.jaguar.com
p. 051

Jung von Matt AG, Germany
www.jvm.de
p. 030

kadavision – new media design, Germany
www.kadavision.de
p. 018

Kleimann & Partner, Germany
www.kleimann-partner.de
p. 072, 080, 081, 088

lateral.net, United Kingdom
www.vapour.org
p. 091

Konstanze Läufer, Germany
www.pictomat.de
p. 093

Index
Digital Media
Internet addresses
CD-ROM
Others

MNO

Masterfood GmbH, Germany
www.twix.de
p. 112, 113

Bruce Mau, USA
www.brucemaudesign.com
p. 039

McAlpine Design Group, Canada
www.afewseconds.com
p. 096

www.mediabasement.com
p. 096

Metadesign, USA
www.fuse98.com
p. 117

Le Monde, France
www.lemonde.fr
p. 095

Montblanc International GmbH, Germany
www.montblanc.com
p. 035

MTV Networks Europe, United Kingdom
www.mtv2.co.uk
p. 075

Mutabor Design, Germany
www.mutabor.de
p. 076, 077, 106, 107, 115, 118

n.a.s.a.2.0 GmbH, Germany
www.nasa20.com
p. 110, 111, 116, 118

Tom Nulens New Media Design, Belgium
www.tomnulens.be
p. 097

www.nomansland.com
p. 058

Ogilvy & Mather, USA
www.ogilvy.com
p. 051

ST

Saatchi & Saatchi, USA
www.saatchi.com
p. 028, 058, 096

Scholz & Friends AG, Germany
www.schloz-and-friends.com
p. 050

Sixt AG, Germany
www.e-sixt.de
p. 078, 079

Ulah Soemitro aka ::Otty::, USA
www.blotty.com
p. 118

Stylepark Aktiengesellschaft, Germany
www.stylepark.com
p. 028

Suction, USA
www.suction.com
p. 116

Swatch AG, Switzerland
www.swatch.com
p.122

SwissOnline AG, Switzerland
www.swissguide.ch
p. 123

Joseph Ternes, USA
www.code-design.com
p. 067

Tresor Records GmbH, Germany
www.tresorberlin.de
p. 041

Troisième Oeil – Design d'Interactions, France
www.3e-oeil.com
p. 018

PR

Pandiscio Co., USA
www.pandiscio.com
p. 104, 105

Paregos, Sweden
www.paregos.se
p. 060, 119

Pixel : Industries – Agency for visual Communication, Germany
www.pixel-industries.com
p. 045

Planet Pixel Funke Hiller Wülfing GBR, Germany
www.planetpixel.de
p. 091

Plazm, USA
www.plazm.com
p. 055

Plumb Design, Inc., USA
www.plumbdesign.com
p. 066

Porsche Design Management GmbH & Co KG, Austria
www.porsche-design.com
p. 051, 066, 138, 139

Relevare Ltd., United Kingdom
www.relevare.com
p. 039

RG Wiesmeier Werbeagentur AG, Germany
www.wiesmeier.de
p. 080, 081

V

Verlag Form GmbH, Germany
www.form.de
p. 028

»emotional_digital«, Verlag Hermann Schmidt Mainz, Germany
www.emodigi.de
p. 057

Veuve Clicquot Ponsardin, France
www.veuve-clicquot.fr
p. 050

Vitra International AG, Switzerland
www.vitra.com
p. 047, 084

Viva Media AG, Germany
www.viva.tv
p. 116

Volkswagen of America, Inc., USA
www.volkswagen.com
p. 136, 137, 143

WXYZ

Waag Society/society for old and new media, Netherlands
www.waag.nl
p. 102, 103

Walker Art Center, USA
www.walkerart.org
p. 087

Wallpaper, United Kingdom
www.wallpaper.com
p. 090

Wilkhahn, Germany
www.wilkhahn.com
p. 037, 039, 065

WM TEAM Werbeagentur, Germany
www.wmteam.de
p. 075

Young & Rubicam Inc., USA
www.yandr.com
p. 116, 125

zellteilung – büro für visuelle leidenschaften, Germany
www.zellteilung.de
p. 045, 094

0-9

24HR International AB, Sweden
www.24hr.se
p. 032

CD-ROMS and others

Das Zifferblatt | Dial-Plate
Andrea Jenzer
with Prof. Michael Klar/Wulf Beck,
Institut für transmediale Gestaltung, UdK Berlin
p. 075

New Beetle interactive
VW | Team-Konzept Informationstechnologien
Berlin, 1999
p. 136, 137, 140–143

**William Forsythe »Innovation Techniques
– A Tool for the Analytical Dance Eye**
ZKM Zentrum für Kunst und Medientechnologie
Karlsruhe, 1994/1999
p. 130, 131

Über die persische Schrift | About Persian Writing
Andrea Jenzer
with Prof. Michael Klar/Wulf Beck,
Institut für transmediale Gestaltung, UdK Berlin
p. 128, 129

Über Geschwindigkeit | About Speed
Anja Denz
with Prof. Michael Klar/Wulf Beck,
Institut für transmediale Gestaltung, UdK Berlin
p. 073

Geschichte der europäischen Musik | History of European Music
Henrietta Schiffer
with Prof. Michael Klar,
Institut für transmediale Gestaltung, UdK Berlin
p. 045

Nokia 6110
Siemens S25
Palm
p. 132, 133

chapter 1

018
Im Dickicht der Sprache | A. J. Storfer
2000 Vorwerk 8

019
FontFont | Typographic Resource
1998 FSI FontShop International

Rejected | Best Rejected Advertising Volume 2
1999 Berlin Press

022
apple macintosh
vogue
the times

023
frog design
neuhaus
lufthansa

024
the x-files

025
kleimann & partner
arch+
the lounge

028
internationales literaturfestival berlin 2001 Katalog | catalogue
2001 Verlag Vorwerk 8

ny times

Standpunkte 5
1996 Hfg Schwäbisch Gmünd

029
Facts & Fakes | Alexander Kluge
2000 Verlag Vorwerk 8

Design Leitfaden
1994 Design Zentrum Hessen

031
Mix, Cuts & Scratches | Westbam mit Rainald Goetz
1997 Merve Verlag Berlin

Facts & Fakes | Alexander Kluge
2000 Verlag Vorwerk 8

Life Style | Bruce Mau
2000 Phaidon Press Limited

Max Dudler – Schule in Berlin-Hohenschönhausen | Dr. Wolfgang Pauser
1998 Gebr. Mann Verlag Berlin

Style & The Family Tunes
No 034 | 10/2000

Mehr oder Weniger Braun-Design im Vergleich
1990 Museum für Kunst und Gewerbe Hamburg

internationales literaturfestival berlin 2001 | programme

Rejected | Best Rejected Advertising Volume 2
1999 Berlin Press

033
form | Zeitschrift für Gestaltung
4/1997 Verlag form

Die Woche

The Great Gigolo Swindle
2000 International DeeJay Gigolo Records

chapter 3

123
Life Style | Bruce Mau
2000 Phaidon Press Limited

Lettre International

chapter 4

136, 140, 141
Catalogue **Der New Beetle**
2001 Volkswagen AG Germany

138
Catalogue **Porsche Design – Golf**
2001 Porsche Design Management GmbH & Co., KG

139
Catalogue **Porsche Design – Eyewear 2001/2002**
2001 Porsche Design Management GmbH & Co., KG

Univers 55

The main text in this book is set in Univers 55 and the headlines in Univers 65.

Apple Chancery	Arial	Avantgarde	Bembo	Bodoni	Clarendon	Courier	ITF Introvert
p. 020	p. 053	p. 020	p. 052	p. 020	p. 024	p. 117	p. 039
				p. 022			p. 053
				p. 039			
				p. 052			

Formata	Futura	Frutiger	Garamond	Gill sans	Helvetica	
p. 020	p. 020	p. 063	p. 020	p. 023	p. 020	p. 053
	p. 023	p. 068	p. 022	p. 053	p. 023	p. 058
	p. 053		p. 052		p. 038	p. 059
			p. 117		p. 039	p. 062
					p. 046	p. 061
					p. 047	p. 069

Laguna Tiapara	Minion	New York	Vera Alternate	Old English	Snell Back
p. 117	p. 061	p. 061	p. 117	p. 020	p. 053
					p. 069

Futura double	Rotis	GF Eccentric Opus	Times	Pixie Plain	Verdana
p. 020	p. 025	p. 020	p. 020	p. 024	p. 024
p. 053			p. 022	p. 053	p. 061
			p. 052		p. 069
			p. 053		p. 117
			p. 061		
			p. 068		

AB

Animation
072, 073, 076, 077, 098, 112, 114, 116,
117, 119, 126–129, 136, 137, 140, 141

Anti-aliasing
058, 068, 069, 077

Banner
126, 127

Base line grid
034, 036, 038–041

Brightness
046, 047, 072, 094

C

Caption
037–039, 129, 140, 141

CD-ROM
059, 073, 078, 128–131, 136–143

Colour contrast
094, 095, 118, 119

Achromatic and chromatic contrast
047
Brightness contrast
046
Cold and cold contrast
047
Combinations of colour tones
047
Complementary contrast
046
Non-colour contrast
046
Quality contrast
046, 048, 051
Warm and cold contrast
047
Warm and warm contrast
047

Colour effects
048, 049

Colour system
044, 045, 046, 072

Additive colour system
044, 072
Subtractive colour system
045, 072

Primary colours
044, 045
Secondary colous
044, 045
Tertiary colours
044

Colour wheel
046

Column height
026, 034

Column length
026, 027

Column width
026, 027, 030, 033, 060, 129

Complementary colours
046

DEF

D-HTML
076, 077

DIN-Format
018, 019

Dramaturgy
114

Edge of page
026

Egyptienne
024

Experimental typeface
024

Feedback
096, 100, 104, 105, 119, 129, 139

Flash
076, 077, 116

Flow chart
078, 080, 082, 107, 114

Foot margin
028

Footnote
038, 040

Frame
076, 096, 097, 119, 126

Front page
072, 119, 122–125

GHIJ

Gap between columns
026, 027

Grid cell
036, 037, 084, 106, 127, 129

Gutter margin
028

Hand-held
131, 132

Headline
024, 025, 038, 039

Head margin
028

HTML
072, 073, 076, 077, 117

Innovative grid solutions
098–113

Fluid grids
108–113
Grid hierarchies
100–107
Linear grids
098, 099

Italic
053, 056, 058, 059, 137, 140, 141

Jump-to-top
121

L

Ladder diagram
078, 079

Leading
026, 027, 034, 040, 066, 140, 141

Letter spacing
022–024, 030, 059, 060, 062, 063

Line length
060, 061, 064, 065, 067

Line slope
059

Line spacing
026, 027, 034, 035, 039, 062–064, 066, 141

Line thickness
020

Loading process
116, 118, 126

Loading time
076, 122, 124, 126, 137, 142

MNO

Main menu
080, 081, 097, 128, 129, 133

Marginal note
038, 040

Mark-up language
072, 076

Mini-screen
131, 132

Mobile phone
131, 132

Navigation
072, 073, 078–093, 098–114, 117–120,
122, 124, 125, 129, 131, 132, 137–143

Network diagram
078, 082, 083

Organiser
131, 132

Outer margin
028

P

Pagination
040, 041, 073, 140, 141

Paging function
121

Paper formats
018, 019

Pixel width
094

Pop-up
077, 096, 097, 127

Position of pictures
036, 072

Programming language
076

Pull-down menu
077, 096, 132, 137

R

Rollover
096

Sans serif
020, 023, 025, 039, 052–055, 058, 141

Saturation
046, 047

Screen typeface
024

Scrolling
066, 067, 076, 089, 101, 102, 105, 106,
113, 120, 131, 139, 141, 143

Semi sans
025

Semi serif
025

Serif
020, 022, 023, 025, 039, 052–055, 058, 068
136

Sub-heading
038, 039, 060, 067

TW

Text quantity
060

Tree diagram
078, 080, 081

Type area
026, 028, 029, 030–034, 036, 041, 078

Typeface
020–027, 030, 036, 038–041, 052–060, 066,
068, 069, 136–138, 143

Type family
025, 059

Type size
022, 024, 026, 027, 030–034, 038, 039, 054,
056, 058–062, 065, 066, 068, 069, 136–138

Word spacing
062, 064, 066

Many thanks to all the companies and designers who made their work available to me.

For their consultation and co-operation I would like to extend my thanks to:
Dr. Bernhard Angerer,
Andreas Böhme, Yan Dehner,
Reinald Gussmann (Photos p. 132, 133)
Prof. Michael Klar and Wulf Beck,
Bernhard Lassahn, Golo Meyer-Thoss,
Silke Obst (Photos p. 21, 38, 39, 132, 133)
Christoph Schnee and Viola Winokan

And a very special thanks to Brian Morris, Publisher of AVA Publishing SA, and to my colleague Eva Fey for her passion, dedication and hard work, all of which were over and above the call of duty. My thanks too to Natalia Price-Cabrera for her hard work and attention to detail, and to Tessa Blakemore for her support.

> grids <